TABLE OF CONTENTS

Page

CHAPTER 1 INTRODUCTION AND BACKGROUND 1

CHAPTER 2 DISCOVERY 9

    The Native People 13
    The First Fruits of Contact: The Impact of Disease 18
    Native Spirituality and Religion 21
    Indian Perspectives on the Europeans 23
    The Land and Commerce 25
    The Dutch and the English 32
    Commercial Entanglements 38
    Rivalry and Murder 44

CHAPTER 3 WAR COMES TO CONNECTICUT 54

    The Murder of John Oldham 59
    An English War Party; 63
    Wrapped in Flames: The Defeat of the Pequot 78

CHAPTER 4 A Chosen People 87

    Indians in Relation to the Puritan Objective 93
    War comes to the Wilderness Zion 97

CHAPTER 5 CULTURES OF WAR 100

    Musketballs and Arrowheads 112
    A Savage Affair: The English Way of War 114
    CONCLUSION 120

BIBLIOGRAPHY 125

CHAPTER 1

INTRODUCTION AND BACKGROUND

In the year 1630 English Puritans established a settlement on the Atlantic coast near present day Salem, Massachusetts. The Massachusetts Bay Colony shared similar, but not identical, Puritan beliefs with their countrymen who had established a small colony on the shore of Cape Cod Bay only a decade prior. During that same period, in what is now southern Connecticut, a powerful regional tribe enjoyed what was probably the zenith of its existence.[1] The Pequot Indians, living along the present day Thames River, were one of the dominant tribes in a densely populated region. Within less than a decade the tribe would be decimated. They would suffer through a disastrous period punctuated by disease, war, subjugation, and absorption. It was the English colonists who unleashed much of this horror on the Pequot people.[2].

This thesis will examine the dominant role that religion, as opposed to commerce, or simple racism, played in the shaping of the English response to the Pequot challenge. The body of this examination consists of four chapters. To provide background and context for the central argument the second and third chapters will examine the converging factors of trade, cultural disruption, and intertribal conflict and their impacts on the political and security environment for the Puritan colonies. Chapter four will discuss in some detail the specific ideology of the Massachusetts Bay Colony Puritans to discover their views on coexistence, compromise, colonization, and conflict. This is significant to understand the profound cultural differences between the Indian and

---

[1] Herbert Milton Sylvester, *Indian Wars of New England,* vol. I (Boston: The Everett Press, 1910), 35.
[2] Alfred A. Cave, *The Pequot War* (Amherst, MA: University of Massachusetts Press, 1996), 43.

European societies that magnified the velocity and impact of specific provocations. It will attempt to describe the cultural terrain that shaped the struggle between native and newcomer, and gave greater force and meaning to otherwise minor events.[3] The fifth chapter will follow thought into action and examine the military mismatch that doomed the Pequot to defeat at the hands of the relatively small English force. Distinct from the obvious technical differences between the parties, there were marked contrasts in the perceptions and expectations of warfare as well as the practice of combat. These differences will further explain the war's final outcome.

The war between the English Colonies of Massachusetts Bay, Plymouth, and Connecticut, and the Pequot Indian tribe was the first organized armed conflict between a northeast native tribe and their newly arrived English neighbors. The suspicion, fear, and hostility of the English towards the native tribes sparked into open conflict in 1637.[4] The central actors, on both sides, believed they were engaged in a struggle for self-preservation. The English brought their own military traditions, forged through centuries of brutal combat, to the colonies and unleashed it on the Pequot, motivated by a religious zeal.[5] During this period each side fell back upon their traditions and creeds to explain the events occurring around them. The war foreshadowed other more extensive campaigns in the struggle for dominance in North America. In this contest between the growing English settlements and the divided and diminished tribes of coastal New England accommodation and compromise were not realistic options.

---

[3] Thomas J. Wertenbaker, *The First Americans 1607-1690* (Chicago: Quadrangle Books, 1955), 91-92.
[4] Alfred A. Cave, "Who Killed John Stone? A Note on the Origins of the Pequot War," *The William and Mary Quarterly*, 3rd Ser., vol.49, no.3 (July1992), 509.
[5] Ibid. 43.

The English colonists in the early seventeenth century were set into a world view framed by their Puritan religious beliefs. The Puritans of Massachusetts Bay Colony adhered to a strict interpretation of their Protestant Christian faith. This influenced nearly all aspects of public and private life, and shaped their understanding of the world around them. Their understanding of their purpose and objectives was framed in religious terms. Those views placed established a barrier between themselves those Indian tribes who adhered to their own set of religious and cultural beliefs.

The Pequot, a proud and powerful tribe, found themselves at odds, politically and culturally, with the expanding English colonies of New England. This fact alone was not enough to place the Pequots in a position to suffer the English wrath. Their own political and economic interests set them on the path for collision. For their part, they were unable to fully understand the perspective and intentions of the English and develop a coherent strategy, or pathway, for dealing with the newcomers. The Pequot were overcome by a storm of catastrophic events which foreshadowed the fate of many other North American Indian tribes.

To answer the primary questions of the thesis the circumstances surrounding the war must be examined. Understanding the English, who were settling the rough coastline of New England in the seventeenth century, means understanding their interpretation of Christianity and how it was firmly woven into their cultural life. Similarly, consideration of the native religious, cultural, and political beliefs enhances our understanding of their actions and responses. These belief systems helped both civilizations map their respective frontiers. Developing a broad view of this "human terrain"[6] can lend perspective to the examination of decisions and outcomes which have shaped our collective past. The same understanding is still relevant today, with refinement, to navigate effectively among the diverse nations of our increasingly crowded world.

The Puritan Separatists, or Pilgrims, who crossed the North Atlantic in the early seventeenth century undertook their journey infused with a sense of divine purpose. They sought to make their homes in the wilderness of North America and establish a free church more aligned with their ideals than the established Church of England. These English pioneers built permanent settlements in New England and interacted with the local tribes. Their reports back to their fellow countrymen further illuminated some of the challenges and opportunities surrounding emigration across the Atlantic.

In North America they found themselves surrounded by alien cultures, and this presented, for the pious, a stumbling block of great magnitude. They understood little about the native religious beliefs except that they were foreign and un-Christian. On the occasions that some observers witnessed native religious rituals and rites they inevitably filtered what they saw through their Puritan experience. The native culture was deeply foreign and not of the "Christian" tradition, which made it misguided at best, satanic at worst.[7] Alfred Cave makes the point in his work on the Pequot War that "The idea of savagery in opposition to civilization was thus an essential part of the English colonizers

---

[6] Max Boot, "Navigating the Human Terrain," *Los Angeles Times*, December 7, 2005, Opinion Page, http://www.cfr.org/publication/9377/navigating_the_human_terrain.html (accessed September 14, 2007).
[7] Cave, 15-18.

sense of identity."[8]

In 1629 a group of nearly four hundred Englishmen sailed for New England. Later in 1630, a fleet of eleven vessels bearing some seven hundred would-be colonists from England arrived off the coast of present day Salem. Prior to their departure from England they had elected a devout lawyer, John Winthrop, as their governor. He would be their advocate, and guide on this journey. These strict Puritans, at odds with the Church of England and despairing of near-term reconciliation sought to physically distance themselves from a country which, they felt, would soon feel the wrath of a righteous and angry God.[9]

Winthrop and others in embarked on the journey felt that they had a unique spiritual charter to create a holy community in this new land. Soon after arrival the colony expanded their footprint, going on to establish a settlement to the south of Salem, Boston, which was to become the seat of government for the fledgling colony. Religious and political discord back in England and the glimmer of commercial opportunity continued to bring people to the new colony.[10]

The merging commercial interests of Europe and the native societies of North America in the first three decades of the seventeenth century have often been identified as the tinder for the conflict between the Indians and the English in New England. The relationship between commerce and conflict must be discussed. Indeed, access to

---

[8] Ibid., 18.

[9] Ezra Hoyt Byington, *The Puritan in England and New England* (Cambridge, University Press, 1896), 87-89.

[10] Bernard Bailyn, "Puritanism and New England Merchants," *The New England Puritans*, Sydney V. James, ed. (New York: Harper and Row Publishers, 1968), 99-101.

European trade goods for the native tribes was not merely a minor cultural adjustment; there were profound effects for these societies. Trade took on expanded political significance for both the Indians and English. Commercial relationships with the English and the Dutch influenced political relations between the tribes. Growing commercialism exacerbated inter-tribal tensions increasing the risks of competition for resources and access.[11] Yet even in times of tension between the native people and the newcomers commerce was freely pursued. Ultimately, consideration of the commercial relations between the English and the native peoples is inadequate to fully explain the ruthless measures the English employed against the Pequot.

It is important to note that the central ideal behind the establishment of these colonies was not economic. These colonies were established by people who viewed their role in the world as God-inspired. The colonists were pragmatic enough to understand the importance that trade would hold for their economic and physical survival. Colonies were, of necessity, commercial ventures as well, not merely havens for those seeking political or spiritual freedom.[12] Yet the transplanted merchants and craftsmen did not operate outside of the cultural framework established and enforced by the Puritan leadership. The Puritans agreed that commerce was subordinate to religion and required a moral underpinning. In Europe centuries of civic and commercial practice preceded the evolution and interpretation of Christian religious doctrines. In the New England colonies the split between the commercial and pious would come over time, as the original founding ideas lost some of their influence. In the beginning however, the religious ideals

---

[11] Wertenbaker, 88-89.
[12] Ronald D. Karr, "Why Should You Be So Furious?: The Violence of the Pequot War," *The Journal of American History* 85, no. 3 (December 1998), 877.

of the Puritans subordinated the commercial aspirations of the community and shaped the civic culture.

When war came the English turned to their clergy, as much as to their military men, for guidance and leadership. The English actions on 26 May 1637 were those traditionally reserved for heretics or infidels. There was a sense of divine mission and justice for many of the English. So when the Englishman John Mason led his force in the burning of the Pequot village at Mystic and the slaughter of its inhabitants, he was acting in the accepted Old Testament mode of a holy instrument of God's wrath and justice.[13] Ultimately it was in this way that the English found greater meaning and justification for their actions.

---

[13] John Mason, "A Brief History of the Pequot War: Especially of the memorable Taking of their Fort at Mistick in Connecticut in 1637". Boston, 1736. In *Major Problems in American Military History*, John W Chambers II and G.Kurt Piehler, eds. Boston and New York: Houghton Mifflin Company, 1999),7-10.

CHAPTER 2

DISCOVERY

Nearly 100 years before the English established their settlements along the rough and rocky coast of Massachusetts Bay, other Europeans scouted the undeveloped shores. An exploration party financed by the French, and led by a hired Italian captain, Giovanni da Verrazano, inspected small segments of what is now the Southern New England coastline. These explorers had sailed up from Virginia and the Carolinas in 1524. All along their route, they traded with the natives, and explored the varied coastline. Following their brief encounters, the French explorers sailed further north eventually reaching Newfoundland before returning home with reports about their voyage. [14]

These reports and accounts given by the early explorers formed the first impressions of an expansive land seemingly awaiting European exploration and settlement. That the New World was inhabited was abundantly clear. However, for the Europeans, North America was a new frontier that seemed to be inhabited by a people markedly different and strange. Explorers' accounts of the natives of these northern lands made them seem quite wild, sometimes threatening, but decidedly alien. However, Europeans saw in the new world an opportunity for access to resources, markets for trade goods and naturally the conversion of the strange indigenous people to Christianity. This developing view was incubated in the minds of Kings, clergy, and colonists alike; and it set the conditions for the political and social interaction between the European colonists

---

[14] Giovanni, Verrazano, *The Voyages of Giovanni da Verrazzano, 1524-1528*, trans. Susan Tarrow Lawrence C. Wroth, ed., http://bc.barnard.columbia.edu/~lgordis/earlyAC/documents/verrazan.htm (accessed 8 November 2007).

and the native peoples they encountered in North America.

Italian explorer Giovanni Verrazano's initial impressions of the land and the people he encountered were relayed in a letter to his sponsor King Francis I of France. In the course of his journey the Indians received the explorers with a mixture of enthusiasm, curiosity, terror, and hostility. This New World seemed open to the Europeans and even the brief descriptions of the natural world must have stoked their curiosity. What is readily apparent in Verrazano's correspondence is that the native people he encountered all along his journey were never considered as the rightful possessors of the land. To a casual observer much of the land appeared to be unused and so was assumed to be unclaimed and available for the taking. The explorer's observations were discussed and filtered through decidedly European perspectives as they made their way through the religious, political, and social circles back in Europe.

Dutch explorer Adraien Block recorded an encounter with a distinct native tribe in the area around present day Hartford, Connecticut in 1614, ninety years after Verrazano's visit.[15] This is widely believed to be the first European contact with the Pequot Indian Tribe. Block's expedition sailed north from Long Island Sound up the Connecticut River into what was the heart of Pequot lands. During this period the Dutch established the settlements and trading posts that comprised their "New Netherlands" colony. The lifeblood of these Dutch settlements was their lucrative trade with the region's Indian tribes.[16] The Pequots' geographic position and regional importance made them

---

[15] Alfred A. Cave, *The Pequot War* (Amherst, MA: University of Massachusetts Press, 1996), 43, 66.
[16] Lois M. Feister, "Linguistic Communication between the Dutch and Indians in New Netherland 1609-1664," *Ethnohistory*, 20, no. 1 (Winter, 1973), 31.

significant among the many tribes with whom the Dutch carried on a lucrative trade in European goods for furs and other commodities.

In the opening decades of the seventeenth century the Pequot, like other regional tribes, found themselves on a path of profound change. Their culture adapted to contact with the Europeans and their way of life altered in ways they struggled to control. Their involvement in the commerce of European traders drew them into a world of competition and conflict. The tribe experienced a period of intensified conflict with neighboring tribes, Dutch traders, and finally with the English.

There were two primary European actors in coastal New England in the early seventeenth century. The English, who initially settled along the shores of what is today Massachusetts, and the Dutch, who established settlements along the Hudson River valley in New York and coastal Connecticut. Relations between the native peoples of the regions and the English were fairly tranquil in the opening decade of the English New England settlement. Colonists scrambled to survive in the challenging North American environment during these early years. The pragmatic realities of making a living in North America came to dominate the various other motivations behind the establishment of these "frontier" colonies.[17]

It would be incorrect to view the English as a monolithic colonial entity. There was tremendous diversity among the English colonies in New England and Virginia. In 1637, at the time of the war with the Pequot, there were four separate political entities. The primary English entity was the growing Massachusetts Bay Colony. To the south of Boston, the smaller but older Plymouth Colony acted independently with some of its own interests and motivations. Still further to the south, and in closer contact with the Narragansett and Pequot tribes, were the fledgling colonies of Rhode Island and Connecticut. Both were closely tied to the Massachusetts Bay Colony. Finally, to the west, distant in the perspective of the day, were the Dutch traders and settlers of New Netherlands, located in present day New York and western Connecticut.

This conflict was not a two-party conflict, with the English settlers battling a native tribe in the wild expanses of the New England interior. Instead, the conflict

---

[17] John, Tebbel and Keith Jennison, *The American Indian Wars* (New York: Harper & Brothers Publishers, 1960), 20-21.

actually involved five separate native tribes with different allegiances and interests: the Pequots, the Narragansetts, the Western Niantic (subordinate to the Pequot), the Block Islanders (allied with the Narragansetts), and the Mohegan tribe (separate from the Pequots but closely related culturally)[18]. Beyond understanding the civic arrangements of the individual tribes they encountered the English also dealt with the challenge of interpreting native economics, cultural norms and religion. Those interpretations then had to fit into their own model to facilitate understanding. The first broad impressions the Europeans had of these people often limited deeper understandings down the road.

The Native People

Until recently there was some dispute about the origins of the Pequot tribe. Specifically there has been some debate concerning the relationship of the Pequot, and their offshoot the Mohegan, with a similarly named tribe in the Hudson River valley, the Mohicans. This view held that the Pequot migrated from the upstate New York area to what is now southern Connecticut approximately twenty years prior to English settlement.[19] With their arrival they displaced some resident tribes and disturbed the socio-political order of the region. The significance of the migration theory however lies in the weight it gave to the belief that the Pequot were an aggressive, opportunistic tribe. However, linguistic studies by Professor Frank G. Speck, among others, have largely

---

[18] Cave, 64-66, 144-152.
[19] Frank Speck and J. Dyneley Prince, "The Modern Pequots and their Language," *American Anthropologist*, 5, No. 2 (April –June 1903), 193.

discredited this theory.[20] Also archaeological evidence indicates that the Pequot were long-term residents of the region and not recent arrivals.[21]

Researchers surmise that prior to European contact, the Pequots, like many neighboring tribes, were a nation of communities and clans. Each settlement, or community, probably represented a distinct political entity with its own interests, and distinct, though similar, processes. Prior to the establishment of trading outposts and colonies most, if not all, Indian villages or settlements were semi-permanent. Seasonal and population demands governed the construction of housing for the tribe.

The native societies in southern New England relied on a mix of agriculture, coastal fishing, and hunting for subsistence. They were politically organized, although not in the European sense of the word. These distinctions later caused misunderstanding and confusion. The location and primary activities of a settlement were tied to seasonal cycles and food availability.[22] There is ample evidence that their interaction with Europeans in the early decades of the seventeenth century began to alter this pattern. The native societies were changed by transatlantic trade just as the western European economies.

The changes to native economies brought by trade modified their need for mobility and their response to the natural environment. Tribes extracted surpluses from the land in terms of animal products and agricultural goods for trade with the English. This increased trade in material goods altered the requirements for mobility among small

---

[20] Speck, 195-199; Cave, 42.
[21] Cave, 40-41.
[22] William Cronon, *Changes in the Land: Indians, Colonists, and the Ecology of New England* (New York: Hill and Wang, 1983), 38-40.

communities.[23] The importance of access to regular, predictable trade took on greater importance. This trend manifested itself in the establishment of permanent settlements. When the Dutch explorers first charted the coastal areas of Connecticut in 1614 they made no mention of the large Pequot villages at Mystic and Weinshauks.[24] Both of these villages were located on hilltop positions probably intended for observation and defense. One of these, *Weinshauks* was reported on the banks of the Pequot river and the second on the west bank of the Mystic River[25]. It is possible that they were overlooked during the exploration however, but that is somewhat unlikely. It is more plausible that the villages were expanded and fortified as trade intensified competition between tribes and with the Europeans.

These villages were larger and more politically significant than other Pequot settlements. Walls or palisades of upright logs anchored in a simple earthwork to support the wall protected these villages.[26] English accounts relate that this village contained about seventy wigwams making it among the largest of Pequot settlements. As any European observer would expect, these villages were the centers of significant political power.

Leadership in a particular village or of a particular clan fell on the person identified as a chief or *sachem*. Quite simply the sachem's role was to provide civic leadership within that given community. European hierarchies were generally more

---

[23] Ibid., 53-54, 82.
[24] Cave, 43.
[25] Kevin A. McBride, "Archeology of the Mashantucket Pequots," in *The Pequots in Southern New England, the Rise and Fall of an American Indian Nation,* Laurence M Hauptman and James D Wherry, eds. (Norman and London: University of Oklahoma Press, 1990), 101.
[26] Ibid., 98-100.

institutionalized than tribal political structures. Each tribe had its own great sachems, and as far as scholars can tell in Pequot society a male member of the community occupied that position. Generally leadership within the tribe was based on lineal kinship with a chief or grand sachem. Researchers qualify this description and assert that other practical factors weighed heavily on the process as well. There is little documentation to trace the lineages and circumstances surrounding leadership succession so the formal details remain murky.[27] What is clear is that the sachem was not a ruler in the same sense that a European king might be. There was a dominant clan or family group but that did not carry the same weight as it might in England, France, or Spain.

Leadership in these societies often passed along familial lines yet by and large they lacked a European-style class structure. William Starna makes the distinction in his essay *Pequots in the Early Seventeenth Century:*

> The historical descriptions of the social organizations of the southern New England Indians, and other data, suggests that the Pequots were an unstratified, ranked, society. Such a social structure is characterized by a limited number of valued or high-status positions, some of which are ascribed, that is, inherited, while others are achieved.[28]

It is likely that within a region there may have been alliances of two or more villages. Individual loyalty to a particular tribe or sachem was much more fluid than in the European nation-state model.[29] Different communities may have shared political leadership. The exact relationships prior to European contact are open to conjecture.

---

[27] William Burton and Richard, Lowenthal, "The First of the Mohegans," *American Ethnologist* 1, no. 4 (November, 1974), 589-599.

[28] William A. Starna, "Pequots in the Early Seventeenth Century," in *The Pequots in Southern New England, the rise and fall of an American Indian Nation,* Laurence M Hauptman and James D Wherry, eds. (Norman and London: University of Oklahoma Press, 1990), 40-41.

[29] Cave, 66.

A grand Sachem, as mentioned in European descriptions, was the most influential leader in a given tribe. They operated politically through the formation of consensus among their people.[30] Within each tribe, of course some sachems had greater influence, and were more far reaching in their influence, than others. Consider as an example the Wampanoag grand sachem, Massasoit, who was often able to wield influence far beyond his own village.[31] Influence was gained through the disposition of favors which, undoubtedly, enhanced the persuasive powers of a leader.

Although the sachem acted in a key role, he did not exercise absolute power. Often there were councils of elders and spiritual figures (Shamans), who shared some of the burden of decision making. The sachem then, in his interaction with these other notable figures, forwarded his agenda or interests as persuasively as possible to gain consensus within the community. So we have to imagine the challenge this presented to the Europeans in general and the English in particular. Even if they had some knowledge of the language or an able interpreter one wonders if they even asked the right questions to discern the leadership structure of the native people. With these challenges it was no wonder that when Europeans dealt with the politics of settlement they organized their observations and understanding of the local tribes according to their familiar "Old World" practices. However, the European tendency to ascribe kingly powers and influence to the tribal sachem could be far off the mark.

Evidence gathered from primary accounts and a careful study of the native culture at the time tells us the Pequot fortified villages at Mystic, or *Missituk,* and Weinshauks

---

[30] Ibid., 43.
[31] John Tebbel and Keith Jennison, *The American Indian Wars* (New York: Harper & Brothers Publishers, 1960), 20.

were the seats of power for two dominant Pequot sachems, Sassacus and Mamoho. This evidence leads many contemporary researchers to assume that a more centralized political and social hierarchy did exist in the Pequot society at the time of the European settlement in New England. Accurately discerning the exact political organization of native tribes is problematic since doing so depends almost entirely on recorded accounts handed down from English, French, or Dutch sources. European accounts are inevitably filtered and translated through the perspective of the European social and political systems. It is therefore easy to see how a European frame of reference could cloud the view of native sociopolitical organization. Nevertheless, current research has attempted to present a more accurate model of native societies and their political make-up.

Even as the English made inroads into southern New England this civic model may have been changing for the Pequot. During their relatively brief interaction with the European colonists, there were likely some significant shifts in the sociopolitical organization of the tribe.[32] Population shifts brought about by epidemics and trade with Europe began to influence the scene. These shifts not only fragmented the tribe but also established some of the conditions for the conflict of 1636-37.

The First Fruits of Contact: The Impact of Disease

Arguably the most tragic effect of increased interaction between Indians and Europeans was the well documented waves of epidemics that scythed through the highly susceptible native populations. The epidemics that came with European contact had an enormous impact on the social structures, and culture of the regional tribes. The apparent

---

[32] Cronon, 87-88.

near-term impacts to this devastation were dramatic population shifts and the attendant social and political disruption. Entire villages ceased to exist. Whole families perished. The scourge of disease did not recognize status or wealth within an afflicted community. Epidemics such as small pox particularly devastated communities that relied upon oral traditions to educate subsequent generations. Sickness and death occurring on such a massive scale shattered traditional tribal social networks.

Typically those living on or near the coast and having the most frequent contact with the Europeans, were the first to suffer the terrible scourge of contact. The southern New England coastline tended to have a significantly greater population density in contrast with the northern coasts of Maine and Canada.[33] Trade arrangements and the change in Indian patterns of life also enhanced this effect. The consolidation of the population into larger, more permanent settlements also facilitated the spread of the deadly viruses that decimated the native populations. Great epidemics raged along the eastern New England coastline from 1616-19. Then in 1633 a small pox epidemic struck the tribes of southern New England and the Pequot were particularly hard hit. They may have suffered a mortality rate of 80 percent.[34] While exact numbers are often in dispute, accounts from witnesses like Plymouth Governor William Bradford and contemporary Thomas Morton attest to the devastation of disease.[35]

The scourge of disease could be interpreted culturally, being seen at once as a blessing or affirmation, or as a horrible divine punishment and demonstration of power.

---

[33] Cronon, 42, 86.
[34] Starna, 33-47.
[35] William Bradford, *Of Plymouth Plantation 1620-1647*, Samuel Eliot Morison, ed. (New York, Alfred A. Knopf Inc., 1970), 270-271.

That interpretation took on great religious significance for the central actors in the early days of European colonization. The trader Thomas Morton relayed the account of one epidemic that raged along the southeastern New England coast early in the century. The account is important for two reasons. It tells us of the devastation caused by the disease but also of the deeper spiritual interpretation of such a plague. It begins with the account of a European captive, likely a Frenchman, held by a Cape Cod tribe.

> One of these five men, outliving the rest, had learned so much of their language as to rebuke them for their bloody deed, saying that God would be angry with them for it, and that he would in his displeasure destroy them; but the savages (it seems boasting of their strength), replied and said, that they were so many that God could not kill them. But contrary-wise, in short time after the hand of God fell heavily upon them, with such a mortal stroke that they died on heaps as they lay in their houses; …. For in a place where many inhabited, there had been but one left to live to tell what became of the rest; the living being (as it seems) not able to bury the dead, they were left for crows, kites and vermin to prey upon. And the bones and skulls upon the several places of their habitations made such a spectacle after my coming into those parts, that, as I travelled in that forest near the Massachusetts, it seemed to me a new found Golgotha.[36]

Despite these scourges the affected tribes retained a flexible system of civic governance. Events that might have provoked a prolonged and bloody contest in Europe allowed the Pequots to fall back on their traditional modes and rights of leadership. It is likely that in some communities entire family groups were removed from leadership positions they may have enjoyed for decades. The native communities produced new leaders and surviving clans continued to adjust to the changes their new associations generated.

---

[36] Thomas Morton, "Manners and Customs of the Indians (of New England), 1637," Oliver J. Thatcher, ed., *The Library of Original Sources,* Vol. V, *9th to 16th Centuried* (Milwaukee: University Research Extension Co., 1907), 360-377, http://www.fordham.Edu/halsall/mod/1637morton.html (accessed August 28, 2007).

The English attempted to study their new neighbors by working to bridge the language and cultural barriers. In turn interaction with European traders and explorers over the years gave some Indians the opportunity to gain familiarity with some European languages and customs.[37] Despite these attempts there remained a significant gulf of understanding between the two peoples. Even in the most generous reports rendered by colonial English and Dutch observers the natural tendency for bias to shape descriptions and assign meanings remained.

Native Spirituality and Religion

For the seventeenth century colonists probably no other topic carried as much cultural weight as issues pertaining to religion. Religious expression and meaning inundated English custom and belief during this period. In the European view the beliefs held by the Indians conveyed a lack of recognizable religion, or worse still, worship and reverence for the diabolic. While observers acknowledged that there were similarities insofar as there was a belief in the afterlife, beyond that there was little common ground regarding religion. It is unsurprising that to the English observers of Indian religious ritual, the performance, and foreign incantations did not evoke images of holiness and a common god. Religious similarities were not readily accepted by the Puritan mind, which did not allow for variation in that regard. In New England at that time there was significant variation in the religious beliefs and practices of Indian tribes in New England. Unlike a familiar European setting, the early visitors to an Indian village would not see a recognizable building devoted to public worship, or familiar religious symbols,

---

[37] Nathaniel Philbrick, *Mayflower, A Story of Courage Community and War* (London: Viking Penguin Group, 2006), 50-54.

or markers. There was no printed language with which they could communicate sacred texts or tradition. Some English observers felt that the Indians were "…in a continual slavish fear" of the devil. This state they attributed to ignorance of the Christian God. Others, more severe in their critique felt that Indian religion and the practice of it were enthusiastically aligned with Satan. [38] In fact even generous observers of Indian culture like Thomas Morton described the Indian spiritual leaders as having a relationship "with the devil" and their priests as "witches"[39]

The culture the European stepped into was an oral culture. Tradition and practice was conveyed by the tribe's holy men or shaman. These figures performed a critical dual function for the community as bearers of the religion, conveyers of its particular theology and as healers. Their incantations relayed both the cultural folklore that underpinned their beliefs and the immediate and practical communication with the perceived spirit world.

The spirit world for the Indian Tribes of New England generally consisted of three "tiers." The first tier contained the spirits, or souls, of men. Native Americans believed that these souls separated from the physical body, in some cases, during life and travel and interacted on some level with the world around them. When the body died, the soul departed and went on to an after-life. The next tier in the spiritual hierarchy was composed of more powerful spirits, or "guardian spirits". These existed in some form for plant and animal species. They also fulfilled some of the roles that Christian tradition ascribed to angels.

The top tier in this construct was occupied by an all-knowing, all-powerful

---

[38] James Axtell, *The Invasion Within, the Contest of Cultures in Colonial North America* (New York: Oxford University Press, 1985), 12-14.

[39] Morton, 360-377.

Creator. Much like the Christian concept of God, this character was seldom felt. Just as in many religious traditions there was a lesser spirit, or evil god, whose presence was acknowledged and mitigated by the individual and the shaman through the elaborate religious rites. Warding off this evil force required frequent intervention in ways which not easily recognizable to a Christian. Interestingly as interaction with Europeans increased and they shared their religion and their germs there was likely a trend toward appeasement or defense against the influence of the *matchemanitou*, or evil god.[40]

Indian Perspectives on the Europeans

The first Europeans to the region came long before the English arrival in 1620. The coastal tribes from Cape Cod down to Connecticut were familiar with the European traders and fishermen who periodically visited the shores. They traded with the English and the French. Some encounters were benign and others bloody. In some cases visitors overstayed their welcome and warriors pursued the newcomers back to their boats. Other times the Europeans seized captives and hauled them back to Europe for profit and fame. In at least two remarkable cases Indians who had journeyed to Europe were able to return to their people. They brought with them a better, if incomplete, understanding of Europeans and some knowledge of their language.[41]

When the early European explorers arrived they overawed their hosts. Given the characteristics of the native religions it was not surprising that the Indians regarded the Europeans in many cases as lesser spirits similar to the guardian spirits of native

---

[40] Axtell, 15-16.
[41] Nathaniel Philbrick, *Mayflower, A Story of Courage Community and War* (London: Viking Penguin Group, 2006), 50-51.

theology. Initially this facilitated early exchanges, communication and for some, conversion. Indian tribes were initially awestruck by the appearance of European ships, "moving islands" and elaborately clothed explorers. The Indians ascribed much of the white man's power to the readily apparent technology they brought with them. Edged weapons, firearms, and vessels immediately come to mind. James Axtell relates how some early explorers witnessed the Indians worshiping their "…guns, knives, and hatchets by blowing sacred smoke over them, as a sacrifice to the spirits within." European mastery of tool making, not to mention the strange and terrible technology revealed in gunpowder, impressed their hosts--for a time. [42]

Naturally, the Indians catalogued and communicated their observations concerning the dress, manners, and customs of the Europeans. Their physical appearance was initially so strange to some Indians that they considered the white, hairy, men another species altogether.[43] Among some tribes there was deferment to the English God, as Roger Williams recorded, "they are easily persuaded, that the God that made English men, is a greater God, because he hath so richly endowed the English above themselves."[44] The European traders, explorers and missionaries of this period were not above using this "wonderment" to their advantage. They leveraged it with some tribes for trade and influence. This novelty did not last for very long and with time and contact the Indians generally overcame their initial state of awe and began to cast a more critical eye at these new visitors to their shores.

---

[42] Axtel, 9-11.
[43] Ibid.,10.
[44] Roger Williams, *A Key into the Language of America,* An Online Electronic Text Edition, http://capecodhistory.us/19th/MHS1794.htm#203a (accessed 8 November, 2007), 205.

When the English arrived and established colonies in New England the regional tribes were already familiarized with the sight and sound of the white men who came from the ocean. Traders had already probed the shores and traded with the tribes there. The coastal tribes near Cape Cod were already decimated by a horrible epidemic and whole villages emptied. They understood that the white men had some strange and terrible power but they had also identified some of the danger the white men brought with them. This is evident in the accounts the Pilgrims give of their initial face-to-face encounter with the Wampanoag Indians at New Plymouth. The parties observed each other for a time then when the English approached them the Indian scouts are reported to have fled.[45] In the case of the Pilgrims, the initial wariness was overcome and a period of pragmatic accommodation between the English and the Wampanoag followed. The Wampanoag tribe accommodated their new neighbors on land depopulated in the epidemics of 1616-19.[46] The English gained their foothold in New England and began to develop and refine their understanding of the land around them and the people who lived there.

The Land and Commerce

In the first decades of the seventeenth century little was known of North America beyond the shoreline and the few rivers explorers had charted. As interaction increased European traders and colonists discovered that these native societies had a civic structure and accepted concepts of ownership and sovereignty. Despite this there was no revision of thought among most influential European thinkers. European governments did not

---

[45] Philbrick, 91-92.
[46] Philbrick, 94-95, 151.

seriously entertain the idea that the native inhabitants had any real dominion worth consideration. Whatever treaties or arrangements the newcomers made to compensate the Indians for land rights were done from a sense of moral obligation, and pragmatism.[47] There was a tremendous assumption on the part of even the most fair-minded European colonist that European "claims" to vast tracts of New World real estate was valid. Some of this belief goes into European views of land use and legitimate jurisdiction and that will be discussed further along in the chapter. Yet colonists sustained these beliefs of legitimacy through the pre-colonial period and into the early colonial period despite the obvious presence of structured, and distinct, societies on that very land.

The Europeans who established their settlements in North America came to a land vastly different from the one they had departed. The land they left had been mastered for centuries. Many of its forests turned to fields, and many fields to villages and towns. The land for hunting, farming, and living was inevitably owned by someone. Furthermore, the continent they departed had states hungry for commodities to fuel their markets. The world that awaited them across the Atlantic was abundantly endowed with great wealth in all things plant, animal, and mineral. All of this on vast expanses of land which belonged to no one as far as the Europeans were concerned. Even use of the term "New England" betrays a decidedly European perspective. For North America was not the "New World" or "New England" to those generations who lived along its shores, hunted in its forests, and tended its soil. Before the Europeans came the native people lived in large numbers

---

[47] Francis Jennings, "Virgin Land and Savage People," *American Quarterly*, 23, no. 4 (October, 1971), 521-522.

and mastered the land to suit their needs.[48]

Indian settlements were often composed of semi-permanent family dwellings, or wigwams. In the land of seemingly endless forests, wood was naturally the dominant building material and these dwellings were constructed of the readily available material often simply logs and bark. They are not known to have constructed the kinds of buildings that the Europeans considered permanent structures. Settlements composed of one to two dozen of these wigwams were not uncommon. Most of these settlements were located along waterways, natural harbors, or coves. Physically there was little to visibly differentiate a village of Pequot Indians from a similar-sized village of Niantic Indians or Narragansett Indians.

The Indians living along the shores and in the forests of what is today New England established methods of farming, fishing, and hunting that supported the establishment of semi-permanent villages, and complex social arrangements. It was routine and practical for tribes to migrate seasonally as Thomas Morton observed "They use not to winter and summer in one place, for that would be a reason to make fuel scarce."[49] So while by and large they did not follow the path of complex societies across the ocean early explorers did recognize that the people inhabiting these coastal areas had a culture, division of labor, and ingenious ability to sustain themselves off of the land.[50] They did not accumulate wealth as the European understood it. They did not store up

---

[48] William Cronon, *Changes in the Land: Indians, Colonists, and the Ecology of New England* (New York: Hill and Wang, 1983), 19-20.
[49] Morton, 362.
[50] John Smith, *A Description of New England 1616,* Paul Royster, ed., An Online Electronic Text Edition, http://digitalcommons.unl.edu/etas/4/[accessed November 8, 2007].17-25.
It is widely accepted that John Smith coined the term "New England" in his reports of the promising region north of the Virginia Colony and New Netherlands.

large surpluses for barter. Gift giving or trade between tribes was important in that it had political meaning. It was not carried out to necessarily enrich one party or the other. In considering some of the differences in perspective it is useful to remember that the Europeans and the Indians both understood the idea of property but comprehended it in markedly different ways.[51]

Among the Indians individual ownership of what William Cronon refers to as "personal goods" was easy to understand. Items were owned because of their utility and they were owned, generally, by the people who made them.[52] For these people there was no strong drive to accumulate excess. This lack of materialism often impressed early visitors.

Among the region's Indian tribes territorial claims could often be haphazard arrangements. There was no written code or custom to follow. This presented a significant stumbling block to European understanding. William Cronon described two important distinctions in his examination of Indian concepts of ownership as they existed in the colonial period. There were two issues involved in consideration of ownership. The first was the concept of individual ownership and the second was the concept as it applied to the collective group or as Cronon distinguished it as "sovereignty" between tribes and villages.[53] Clans, because of kinship association, may have held claims that crossed from village to village and were not strictly localized. So as Cronon identifies "even the village is sometimes an arbitrary unit in which to analyze property rights: ownership and sovereignty among Indian peoples could shade into each other in a way Europeans had

---

[51] Ibid., 80.
[52] Cronon, 61.
[53] Cronon., 58.

trouble understanding." Some English observers did attempt to place the Indian concepts within the framework of their own understanding. The rights to territory, or property were valid only when recognized by surrounding communities.[54]

Even with this recognition European and Native American ownership norms were not in synch. Possession was often seasonal and tied to a particular use for that land. "What the Indians owned- or, more precisely, what their villages gave them claim to- was not the land but the things that were on the land during the various seasons of the year."[55] This principle included agricultural land, fishing areas, or even clam banks. There was a mutually held understanding that supported common use in some cases. It would have been possible for a particularly fruitful seasonal fishing site or hunting area to have the people from multiple villages or clans sharing access to the site. The guiding principle seems to have been what you killed or pulled from the water was yours.[56] This did not mean that these were societies free from the vice of greed. In fact there seems to be some strong evidence that the growth of trade with the Europeans presented a new variable that may have inflamed this vice.

By 1620 European trade became more common in southern New England. At this time Native Americans viewed commercial exchange with the Europeans as a means to gain greater status through material wealth, and access. Within only a few years of

---

[54] Ibid., 58-59.
[55] Ibid., 65.
[56] Cronon., 63-64.

contact it became apparent that the tribes trading with the Europeans were in competition in ways they had not experienced in their cultural memory.[57]

With the expansion of commerce between European traders and Indian tribes the market for desirable goods evolved. As traders encountered tribes who had finished products already in hand, they sought out other goods to offer in exchange for the raw materials the economic system demanded. Strings of marine shell beads known as Wampumpeag, or Wampum, had already established itself as an exchangeable item by the time the Europeans arrived on the scene. Trade with the Europeans saw the demand for this commodity balloon. The origin of the trade good known as Wampum is not clear. What is clear is that its use expanded with the arrival of the European traders and its significance as a form of currency, with utility for the trading parties, grew accordingly. The English trader Thomas Morton remarked on its use in his account, "We have used to sell any of our commodities for this *Wampampeak [sic]*, because we know we can have beaver again of them for it: and these beads are current in all the parts of New England, from one end of the coast to the other."[58] This "currency" also had a deeper significance for the Indians than it did the Europeans.

In its broader significance Wampum was understood by some to possess supernatural qualities and it took on an importance greater than a simple tool of exchange. It was utilized almost universally as an exchange item. The multitude of uses included gift giving, ransom for captives, ornamentation, payment for religious services

---

[57] Lynn Cesi, "Wampum as a Peripheral Resource in the Seventeenth-Century World System," in *The Pequots in Southern New England, the Rise and Fall of an American Indian Nation,* Laurence M Hauptman and James D Wherry, eds. (Norman and London: University of Oklahoma Press, 1990), 55-60.
[58] Thomas Morton and Oliver J. Thatcher, eds., *The Library of Original Sources*, vol. V, *9th to 16th Centuries* (Milwaukee: University Research Extension Co., 1907), 360-377.

or healing, or as tribute to key sachems. Wampum's utility was its transportability and this increased its value in exchange. Indeed the good seemed have great utility in a multitude of circumstances. [59]

Although it has been simply described as colored beads strung together, this is not completely accurate. Actual trade wampum was crafted from the shell of small marine animals and hard shelled clams, or *quahog*. Prior to the arrival of Europeans and the trade of metal tools the Wampum was made using less precise stone tools. Wampum was hollowed, shaped, and then strung, bead-like. These strings were easily fashioned into belt-like strips that facilitated easy transport and storage. The larger the belt of wampum the more value it held. The source of the raw material for Wampum belts, the quahog, could be found along the New England coastline from the south edge of Cape Cod west along southern Connecticut and Long Island. So as trade, through the hands of the Europeans, increased along the coastline and into the interior of the Northeast, the demand for the raw materials of this trade item naturally increased.[60]

The Dutch colonial experience illustrates how this expansion occurred in the early colonial period. The Dutch, trading north into the interior with Iroquois tribes and east into Connecticut with the Algonquians, quickly realized the value of the beaded belts. As markets became saturated with finished goods and the demand for such goods diminished, the Dutch traders saw the great utility in the prized Wampum. With demand for raw materials, primarily furs, on the rise, the Dutch drew the bead producers more

---

[59] Cronon, 95.
[60] Lynn, 49-50.

tightly into the exchange loop that started to flourish in the 1620s.[61]

Along the coast the gathering, processing, and production of Wampum increased. In exchange, the coastal tribes, particularly dominant ones like the Pequot or Narragansett, gained access to furs and finished goods.[62] Such goods were then added to the exchange circle among the tribes. The Dutch and upland tribes then exchanged the finished Wampum for the "harvested" furs their market demanded. By 1623 the trade with the Europeans, and the dominance of that trade, was becoming a motivating force for conflict within and between native tribes. This cycle of interaction with the Europeans quickly increased the intensity of competition.

The Dutch and the English

Like the other major players in the expanding European global trade game during the seventeenth century, the Dutch sought to gain a foothold in the vast, unexploited, lands across the Atlantic. A series of positive reports from their explorers encouraged the Netherlands' government to support the establishment of a colony, or province, at the mouth of the Hudson River. The Dutch government granted the Dutch West India Company a twenty-four year trading monopoly in North America. By 1623 the company organized its first permanent trading settlements as well as a headquarters settlement. Expansion from their toe-hold was rapid with its small trading settlements appearing in the north, up the Hudson River valley, and east into "New England" and Long Island. With the Dutch West India Company's administrative base in New Amsterdam, present

---

[61] Cronon, 95-96.
[62] Bradford, 203.

day New York, the colonial leaders of the New Netherlands colony oversaw an expanding footprint that was thinly settled but which conducted a lucrative trade with the numerous native tribes it encountered.[63]

The Dutch were hardly the only Europeans finding their way into what explorer Captain John Smith referred to as "New England" in the first decades of the century.[64] A confluence of events drew more Englishmen to the shores of New England less than five years after John Smith's report on the suitability of New England for colonization. This process found willing participants among some of the religious non-conformists who also sought a new start, a new home for themselves and their families. Investors eagerly supported claims to lands in the New World, hoping for abundant returns. In return they invested in brave and, some could argue, desperate souls on their journey to establish colonies in North America.

To the northeast of the Dutch settlements the arrival of approximately 102 Englishmen on the shores of present day Massachusetts in 1620 marked the start of the second English settlement on the shores of North America.[65] These settlers, known in American History as the Pilgrims, but among their contemporaries as Non-conformists or Separatists, had renounced their connections with the established Church of England. They favored simple, unadorned forms of worship and they held a decided aversion to any of the trappings associated with the Roman Catholic Church. Their roots as a movement went back to the closing decades of the sixteenth century when their founder,

---

[63] Louis Jordan, "*The Dutch in America: From Discovery to the First Settlement, 1609-1621,*" http://www.coins.nd.edu/ColCoin/ColCoinIntros/NNHistory.html (accessed 10 November, 2007).

[64] John Smith, *A Description of New England (1616)*, Paul Royster, ed., An Online Electronic Text Edition, http://digitalcommons.unl.edu/etas/4/ (accessed November 8, 2007).

[65] Philbrick, 43, 89.

Robert Browne, determined that the established Church of England failed to follow the letter and spirit of the Gospels. Their discontent was such that they sought a complete break with the national church. This was not an accepted course of action in the political environment of the day. The movement found itself outlawed, pursued, and persecuted in their home country.[66] After facing years of state-sanctioned persecution some of the Separatists sought a new home in Holland.

In Holland they found a more permissive environment where they practiced their religion freely. This was not an easy transition for these Englishmen who undoubtedly clung to the hope of returning home someday. As their time in the Netherlands wore on many English-born Separatists bowed under the rough life as exiles. They feared that their children were trapped into a harsh life with limited options and great risks. This realization was perhaps the final straw for some of these English exiles and they began to consider making another move to start over again.[67] After much deliberation, they considered the New World the only location that might offer them the best opportunity to begin a new life with some liberty to establish a community structured according to their values. So between 1619 and 1620 the Separatists started research on the possibility of establishing a settlement in North America. The first band of English to make this journey departed with a mix of optimism and trepidation in September 1620.[68]

Following a difficult cross ocean voyage of nearly two months the *Mayflower* sighted land. It is difficult today to understand the conflicting emotions of those first

---

[66] Ezra Hoyt Byington, *The Puritan in England and New England* (Cambridge: University Press, 1896), 9-17.
[67] Bradford, 23-25.
[68] Philbrick, 18-31.

Englishmen coming to establish their new life. William Bradford gives us some indication of their initial relief as they looked upon the new continent in his history, *Of Plymouth Plantation*. Yet as their ships drew within view of the shoreline he also provides us with some sense of the immediate concerns this "New World" presented to the earliest colonists.

> Besides what could they see but a hideous and desolate wilderness, full of wild beasts and wild men- and what multitudes there might be of them they knew not. Neither could they, as it were, go up to the top of Pisgah to view from the wilderness a more a more goodly country to feed their hopes; for which way soever [sic] they turned their eyes (save upwards to the heavens) they could have little solace or content in respect to outward objects.[69]

At the shoreline their perceptions collided with the reality of their predicament. Surely they departed largely encouraged by reports of a land rich with resources to sustain them and commodities to make them profitable. Yet in November, 1620 the land they looked on from the deck of the *Mayflower* gave them little comfort beyond the assurance that their sea voyage was over. The familiar was behind them. Here, as Bradford related there were, "…no friends to welcome them nor inns to entertain or refresh their weather beaten bodies; no houses or much less towns to repair to, to seek for succor."[70] They understood that ahead of them were numerous trials and challenges not least of which was dealing with the "savage" native people they had heard and read of, and so expected to encounter.[71]

Arriving late in the year, the newcomers had little opportunity or ability to

---

[69] William Bradford, *Of Plymouth Plantation,* 1620-1647, Samuel Eliot Morison, ed. (New York,:Alfred A. Knopf Inc., 1970), 62.
[70] Cave,61
[71] Bradford, 26.

establish themselves in the rough new land and over the course of the ensuing winter nearly half of the colonists perished. The surviving Pilgrims attempted to revive their flagging colony in the spring of 1621.[72] To their good fortune they encountered tribal leaders who not only lacked the ability or desire to resist their settlement but also seemed amendable to the idea of the settlement of this "new" tribe. The Indians and the Pilgrims signed a Treaty of Peace that same spring.[73] Disease had so diminished the coastal Indian population that the Wampanoag could cede this land without disruption to their remaining settlements.

In the eyes of the "New Plymouth" colony their survival was only superficially due to the assistance of the local Indians but rather as a sign of God's divine favor on their endeavor.[74] This sense of divine purpose and direction pervaded the thinking of these English colonists. The newcomers resisted the idea that there was genuine goodwill at the heart of the aid. Instead, they saw their good fortune as God-driven. This was natural in the context of their view of themselves as a chosen people, sent by their God, to the darker regions of the earth to civilize and contend with those diabolic forces that were ever present away from the true community of the Protestant church. As Bradford reflected on the survival of the tiny colony through the winter in the midst of a multitude of "barbarous and most treacherous" natives he concluded that the "powerful hand of the Lord did protect them."[75]

By the end of the decade, the survival and success of the Pilgrim colony in

---

[72] Philbrick, 81-85.
[73] Ibid., 79-81.
[74] Bradford, 89,102.
[75] Ibid., 83.

Plymouth encouraged others in England to seek relocation to New England.[76] Puritan communities in England were driven by their dissent with the direction and practices of the Church of England. These Puritans differed with their Separatist brethren regarding their relationship with the Church of England. They rejected elements of the church's practice but chose to maintain a connection with the Church of England. Nevertheless, their resistance to some aspects of church doctrine earned them persecution under some of the same harsh rules leveled against the Separatists.[77]

These non-conformists sought to distance themselves from a country which, they felt, would soon feel the wrath of a righteous and angry God. Doctor Leonard Bacon relays the parting words of Mr. Higginson, a church father, as they departed England for the New England, "We do not go to New England as Separatists from the Church of England, though we cannot but separate from the corruptions of it; but we go to practice the positive part of the Church reformation, and to propagate the Gospel in America."[78] In 1629 a group of nearly four hundred Englishmen sailed for Massachusetts. Later in 1630, a fleet of eleven vessels bearing some seven hundred would-be colonists from England arrived off the coast of present day Salem. Prior to their departure from England they had elected a devout lawyer, John Winthrop, as their governor.

Winthrop and others in the new community felt that they had a unique spiritual charter to create a holy community in this new land. Much like their separatist neighbors to the south the newcomers had a challenging first winter, suffering some two hundred deaths. The following spring some people, broken by their first experiences, returned to

---

[76] Byington, 86.
[77] Ibid, 87-88.
[78] Byington, 88.

England. The remainder expanded their footprint, going on to establish a settlement to the south, Boston, which became the seat of government for the fledgling colony. Religious tensions and the glimmer of commercial opportunity continued to lure settlers from Britain. By the year 1631 there were approximately two thousand members of the Massachusetts Bay Colony.[79] Within the span of a few years the Massachusetts Bay colony outpaced the much smaller settlement of the Separatists to the south.

The founders of the Puritan community in Salem elected to develop their church in a similar fashion to the church in Plymouth Colony. However the two colonies did differ in their other social institutions. In their political structure the Plymouth colony was more democratic, and had few traces of the "Old World" class structure. The colonies to the north retained more of the structure and institutions of England. In particular the right to suffrage was more restricted, specifically to members of the church, the Independent Congregational Churches. Some thought was given to a proposal that Puritan noblemen should settle in Massachusetts and enjoy a permanent place in government. This thought did not take root but as Byington identifies in his study of the two Puritan colonies, many of these tendencies reflect the background of the participants. The Separatists were more diverse, some having spent years abroad in Holland. In contrast the Puritans of the Massachusetts Bay colony came straight out of English society.[80]

Commercial Entanglements

These English settlements were not merely havens for religious non-conformists.

---

[79] Herbert Milton Sylvester, *Indian Wars of New England,* vol. I (Boston: The Everett Press, 1910), 189.; *The Columbia Encyclopedia*, 6th ed., s.v. "Winthrop, John, 1588-1649, governor of Massachusetts Bay colony."
[80] Byington, 98-101.

The colonies were commercial ventures as well. Each settlement had creditors back in England. The colonists were pragmatic enough to understand the importance that trade held for their economic survival. Their populations were sufficiently small enough that they did not require land as much as they required commerce. The Plymouth colonists struck out and made contact with other tribes further to the south and west. In 1623 the Pilgrims made contact with a tribe in present day Rhode Island, the Narragansett. The results of their first contact were largely disappointing. The Narragansett had already obtained European trade goods from the Dutch, who were aggressively trading into the interior of Connecticut and along the southern coastline as far east as Rhode Island at this point.[81] Additionally the Narragansett were becoming a political problem and a potential threat to the Plymouth Colony and the tribes along the eastern coast.[82] There was increasing pressure on the Pilgrims of the Plymouth colony that they would have to attend to matters of commerce to give a return to their investors. It became readily apparent to the Pilgrims that their commercial interests forced them to have some dealings with the Dutch.

By 1623 the trade with the Europeans, and the dominance of that trade, became a motivating force for conflict within and between native tribes. This cycle of interaction with the Europeans quickly increased the intensity of competition. As discussed, within most tribal groups, the sachem who leveraged the trade system to provide tokens, or wealth, for supporters, naturally gained prestige and influence. Such influence remained essential to leadership within the consensus-driven political structure of the tribe. It is

---

[81] Bradford, 139.
[82] Philbrick, 126-127.

apparent that the Pequot were quick to discern some of these benefits and actively sought out ways to monopolize the developing trade with the Dutch. For their part the Dutch recognized the growing value of Wampum beads and actively courted the Pequot for their access to the raw materials and their river access to interior tribes. Pequot leaders developed a greater thirst for wealth and subdued weaker tribes through intimidation and, when required, armed conflict.[83]

Once subdued, the lesser tribe paid tribute, often in the form of Wampum, to the Pequot. In under a decade their tribal reach extended across Long Island Sound to the shores of Long Island. The Pequot thirst for wealth and power motivated them to expand their grip on access to raw materials.[84] Looking back, we can see how their expanded role now propelled the tribe into the play-for-keeps world of European politics. It is likely that their desire to compete with the other tribes and with the Europeans firmly planted the seeds of their destruction.

The Dutch were not without competition for trade with the native peoples in southern New England. The English colonies of Plymouth and Massachusetts Bay, seeking sought to pay off the creditors who financed their migration. The colonies also sought greater involvement in the lucrative fur trade to expand their profits. While they still held their religious convictions close, this did not stop them from conducting commerce with the Indians when a profit could be realized.

The Pilgrims were the first to work their way west with their foray to trade with the Narragansett. The Dutch soon learned of this adventure and recognizing the challenge

---

[83] Cave, 49-50.
[84] Ceci, 48-68.

of competing with another European power, sought to dissuade the English from this pursuit. The English communication with the Dutch from Governor Bradford went so far as to remind the Dutch that the English King was the rightful sovereign to all of North America.[85] This bold claim spoke of the disregard the English had for the native peoples. Unremarkably, the Dutch rejected such a claim. In 1627, the Dutch sent an envoy to Plymouth Plantation, a trader named Isaak de Reasieres, to report on the situation. De Reasieres sought to offer the English incentives to turn away from the trading frontier in southern New England. He introduced the Pilgrims to the utility of Wampum for trade with the tribes and persuaded the English to establish trading posts to the North, on the Kennebec River. There the English traded for pelts, initially with corn, then later with the Dutch-supplied Wampum. This diverted the English, but only for a short period.[86]

The Narragansett tribe was perhaps the only viable counterweight to the consolidation of Pequot power in Southern New England in the 1620s and 30s. When trade with the Europeans became the going concern in their small part of the world, the counterparts of European contact, disease and conflict, closely followed. When disease decimated the coastal tribes to their east and south, the Narragansett were spared. This opened the door to their brief ascendancy in the region. Smaller and weaker tribes attributed the strength of the Narragansett and good fortune to spiritual forces. This view was not entirely unlike the religious interpretation of events common with the English.

The Narragansett began a trading relationship with their nearest European neighbors, the English at the Plymouth colony. This growing relationship, based as it was

---

[85] Cave, 54. ; *Governor William Bradford's Letter Book,* (Bedford Massachusetts: Bedford Books, 2001), 30-32.
[86] Cave, 54-57.

on a desire for profit rather than trust, again turned the English toward the regions of Southern New England. Therefore, like the Pequot, the Narragansett grew in influence and power. Lesser tribes such as the Maniseans, from Block Island, the Cowesets, Nipmucs, and eastern Niantic, fell into the Narragansett sphere of influence and became tributaries.[87] With their rise the Narragansett ambitions came into conflict with their powerful neighbors, the Pequots.

The Narragansett proved to be a potent tribe that refused to be cowed into submission by the large and prosperous Pequots.[88] This evolved into a state of conflict between the two tribes that spanned nearly five years as the two wrestled for dominance of the resources and trading access in southern New England. Little primary source material exists to provide details about the Pequot-Narragansett conflict. It can be surmised that they waged war, at least initially, in much the same way as other native tribes of the region.

The contrasting military traditions of the Europeans and the New England Indians will be discussed at greater length in another chapter. However, a few points are worth noting here. First, in general, warfare consisted of small sporadic actions, raids for captives or to terrorize a village. Revenge killings were also commonplace. On rare occasions, the natives may have fought pitched battles but these were limited by the size of their war parties and their technology. While individual combat could at times be lethal the occasion for it was limited. A tribe did not enter into conflict in the same way European states or factions might. Often the *war party* was a voluntary undertaking and

---

[87] Ibid., 63-64.
[88] Sylvester, 199.

not necessarily led by the political leader of the community.[89] The results of combat were often far less decisive than what was seen in the combat of mass armies in Europe. Roger Williams, perhaps one of the most balanced observers of the native tribes at the time of the Pequot War, gives us a brief description of combat between tribes:

> Their Warres [sic] are farre lesse bloudy [sic], and devouring then the cruell [sic] Warres of Europe; and seldome [sic] twenty slaine in a picht [sic] field: partly because when they fight in a wood every tree is a Bucklar [shield]." "When they fight in a plaine [sic], they fight with leaping and dancing, that seldome [sic] an Arrow hits, and when a man is wounded, unlesse [sic] he that shot followes upon the wounded, they soone [sic] retire and save the wounded: and yet having no Swords, nor Guns, all that are slaine [sic] are commonly slain with great Valor and Courage: for the Conquerour [sic] ventures into the thickest, and brings away the head of his Enemy.[90]

While these conflicts were not as dramatically violent or destructive as European wars their impact should not be shunted aside too casually. The Indian males who made up the war party were important providers for their communities; they were not surplus manpower for their village or tribe. Their loss had a detrimental impact on the welfare of their tribe or clan. In the years of European colonization when populations faced reductions from disease, losses from warfare were particularly difficult to absorb.

It is also worth noting that the trade in firearms to some of the tribes started to impact the conduct of combat. With matchlock weapons making their way into the hands of New England Indians some now had a weapon that could inflict more damage with

---

[89] James Axtel, *"The English Colonial Impact on Indian Culture,"* in *The European and the Indian*, (New York: Oxford University Press, 1981), http://www.lehman.cuny.edu//deanedu/litstudies/techprojects/panyc00/axtefram.htm (accessed 17 October 200).

[90] Roger Williams, "A Key into the Language of America," in *Major Problems in American Military History*, John W Chambers II and G.Kurt Piehler, ed. (Boston and New York: Houghton Mifflin Company, 1999), 46

much less investment in terms of individual skill if used correctly. The mere presence of firearms on a field of battle, even when inexpertly wielded, had great impact. For the native peoples who viewed many European goods as imbued with a spiritual, or supernatural, power the flash and boom of the matchlock was a powerful omen and potent in battle. It is unsurprising then that trade in weapons, although not holding the importance as trade in Wampum, had taken on greater significance for the tribes.[91] Naturally this was yet another good that the Indians could only obtain from European traders. Though there are some accounts of fisherman and traders not associated with the colonies trading in weapons it is not clear what was being traded but it is clear that the value placed on the trade in weaponry only deepened the reliance of the native tribes on contact with the Europeans. This alarmed some among the English.[92]

Rivalry and Murder

The English trade shifted back toward the Narragansett early in the 1630s stoking the growing Anglo-Dutch rivalry. The Dutch, for their part, worked hard to spread their trade outposts deeper into English-claimed territory. In 1633 the Dutch established a fortified trading outpost near present day Hartford and named it House of Good Hope. This outpost placed them in closer contact with the Connecticut River tribes and the Pequot. The English from the Plymouth colony established their own outpost that same year a short distance to the north of the Dutch outpost.[93] Massachusetts Bay Colony,

---

[91] Cronon, 95-96.
[92] Bradford, *Governor William Bradford's Letter Book*, 43.
[93] Sylvester, 186-196.

struggling with issues of its own at the time, nevertheless saw fit to establish its own outpost just to the south.[94] So with the two European powers, Dutch and English, competing for the attention and trade the two dominant native tribes, the Pequot and the Narragansett, contended for access to these trade opportunities. The animosity and competition ignited the fuse that eventually led to the conflict of 1637.

    The conflict between the Pequot and the Narragansett soon directly involved the Europeans. Prior to 1633 the Dutch Commander of the post, Jacob Van Curler, had worked with the Pequot to allow more direct access to members from other tribes to the new trading post.[95] It was, after all, in their interests to trade directly with these tribes rather than through the Pequot exclusively. The Pequot initially agreed to the Dutch proposal to open access to the post. The exact terms and incentives for the agreement are not known, but it is clear that only the Dutch viewed it as a binding agreement. The Pequot violated this understanding by killing several people from another tribe who came to the post to trade with the Dutch.[96] In his book on the war, Alfred Cave argues that the victims were quite likely Narragansetts. He indicates the likelihood based on the open and known rivalry between the two tribes at the time. Other authors, such as Richard Radune, make the case that a tributary tribe may have sought to trade directly with the Dutch themselves, in violation of agreements with the Pequot. It is not a matter of record which tribe the victims came from. The Dutch accounts are clear that the Pequot were the

---

[94] Richard Radune, *Pequot Plantation-The Story of an Early Colonial Settlement* (Branford, Connecticut: Research in Time Publications, 2005), 20-21.
[95] Cave, 57-58.
[96] Cave, "Who Killed John Stone? A Note on the Origins of the Pequot War," *The William and Mary Quarterly*, 3rd ser., vol. 49, no. 3 (July 1992), 513.; Sylvester,186-196.

perpetrators. This incident infuriated Van Curler. The Dutch responded in a manner they supposed the Pequot would have no difficulty interpreting.

The Pequot grand-sachem Tatobem, probably the most politically powerful Pequot sachem at the time, came to the trading post at some point soon after the murders. In large measure, his power held the rivalry of subordinates in check, and some semblance of unity within the tribe. The Dutch undoubtedly had some awareness of his significance to the Pequot and chose him as the target for their retribution. Tatobem boarded a Dutch vessel and was promptly seized and held for a ransom. The Dutch informed his companions that if they wanted to have their leader back alive, they needed to pay a ransom of a bushel of Wampum. The Pequot paid the ransom, but the Dutch murdered Tatobem anyhow.[97]

The murder of Tatobem ruptured the Dutch-Pequot trade alliance. It set into motion a dangerous series of events that led to the fracturing of the Pequot nation, and ultimately, war between the Pequot and an alliance of English and native tribes. The Pequot probably considered the murder of one of their grand sachems as an ill omen for the power and unity of their tribe.[98] Some time that same year, 1633, the wave of illness, that decimated distant coastal tribes earlier in the century found its way into the villages of the Pequot nation.[99]

In the winter of 1633-34, smallpox struck with its usual power against the Pequot people and other tribes along the Connecticut River valley. While the exact rate of mortality is not known, it can be reliably guessed. Nearly two thirds of the tribe perished

---

[97] Cave, 58-59.
[98] Ibid., 68.
[99] Ibid., 43

from a pre-epidemic population of approximately 16,000.[100] This undoubtedly tore holes in the tribal society that took generations to recover from. The Pequot did not have that kind of time. There would be no recovery.

By any measure the blow to the native nations afflicted by smallpox in 1633-34 must have been severe. The native people had no natural resistance to these new epidemics. Old and young perished, tribal elders, shamans, and sachems were all likely victims. The 1633 epidemic decimated the Pequot population in the same ways it had tribes in coastal Massachusetts in 1616-19.[101] This undoubtedly presented enormous challenges for the communities as they dealt with the natural and man-made influences acting on them. Amid this turmoil within the Pequot nation, their differences with the people who identified themselves as Mohegan grew deeper.

Many scholars dealing with the North American tribes identify the Mohegan as a branch of the Pequot tribe. The common assertion is that a split occurred sometime in the first decades of the seventeenth century. Some others, like Cave, assert that the Mohegan were most likely a separate tribe, closely tied by marriage and blood lines to the Pequot.[102] For the purposes of this examination of the war in 1637 it is sufficient to understand that by the mid-1630s the tribes operated as separate political entities with divergent interests and allegiances.

The Mohegan grand sachem, Uncas, was viewed as a contender for leadership within the Pequot tribe following the death of Tatobem. Ultimately, the selection fell not to Uncas, but to Sassacus, who was Tatobem's son. Tatobem was Uncas's father-in-law,

---

[100] Ibid., 43.
[101] Morton, 360-377.
[102] Sylvester, 246-247.

and so he was further from the blood line, and without the support of key tribal figures. This sealed the split between the peoples. As tensions increased between the Pequot and the English, Uncas, often described as an opportunist, aligned himself more closely with the English.[103]

In the autumn of 1633 the Pequot were already in decline. Against the backdrop of a ravaging disease the tribe undoubtedly felt the pressure of a simmering conflict with the Narragansett and their allies. Tatobem had been murdered by the Dutch when the tribe required stable leadership. During the ensuing dispute to determine who would assume Tatobem's position, the tribe suffered another division as the sachem Uncas and his supporters chose, once and for all, to separate themselves from the Pequot. Undoubtedly the Dutch, and to a lesser extent perhaps the Plymouth English, had some insight into the turmoil occurring with some of their native trading partners. It is not clear if the Dutch or English fully understood the impact of the tribe's internal turmoil.[104]

The murder of Tatobem ruptured the relations with the Dutch, so it is doubtful that any meaningful intelligence passed on to them. English relations were naturally more mature with the tribes geographically closer to their settlements along the Massachusetts coast. Neither of the English colonies conducted any meaningful business with the Pequot by late 1633. Therefore, all of the intelligence the English had of the Pequot tribe came from partisan sources. The Narragansett, Eastern Niantic, Mohegan and other River valley tribes passed on biased information to the English, already predisposed to assume the worst treachery from the natives. Furthermore, the Dutch, in the wake of their clashes

---

[103] Cave, 66-68.; Sylvester, 247.
[104] William Burton and Richard Lowenthal, 595-597.

with the Pequot, were no more likely to pass on unbiased information about the tribe. The Pequot themselves made a miscalculation in 1634 that only added one more layer to the growing list of negative impressions the English gained of this "warlike" tribe to their southwest.[105]

Late in 1633 the English trader, Jonathan Stone, and his small crew sailed from Boston bound for points south. Most likely, he was headed to New Amsterdam or the Virginia colony. Stone was, after all, from the Virginia colony, not Boston. He ran afoul of the authorities in both the Plymouth and Massachusetts Bay colonies so it is likely that he was compelled to leave.[106] His course took him into Long Island Sound toward the Dutch Colony of New Amsterdam. He decided at some point to make a short halt in the voyage at the mouth of the Connecticut River. It was there that the Pequots acted on what they perceived as an opportunity to avenge the death of their sachem Tatobem by taking the lives of some of the treacherous Europeans.

For reasons unknown Stone and his crew proceeded slightly upriver. The Pequot party was believed to have stalked the small boat as it proceeded. The ship anchored for the night and a portion of the crew came ashore. It was at this point that the Indians moved against the Englishmen. One party killed the crewmen on the shore, and freed two native captives who were probably Niantic seized to act as guides. The other half of the raiding party boarded the boat where they killed Stone, his crew, and set fire to the craft. In the months and years after the event this was the story given to the English by the Pequot. The initial report filtered back to the English with a few months, but given

---

[105] Radune, 18-21.
[106] Bradford, 268-269.

Stone's reputation among the English of New England, there was little surprise or outrage.[107]

As Cave points out in his text, it is interesting to note that the Pequot never denied their role in the deaths of Stone and his crew. The Pequot asserted however that they supposed the Englishmen to be Dutch and therefore legitimate targets for retaliation according to their custom.[108] The initial assertions were delivered by ambassadors from the Pequot tribe who arrived in Boston in October 1634. The visitors came bearing wampum belts and promised more. The stated purpose for their visit was to seek the friendship of the English. The initial visit was cordial enough but the Massachusetts Bay Colony magistrates would not negotiate with the emissaries with a sachem or someone of similar rank from the tribe. A period of weeks later two sachem appeared before the Puritan magistrates to develop details of the arrangement.[109]

The Pequot ambassadors requested that the English help mediate an end to the war with the Narragansett. This instance would have perhaps presented a good indicator of the pressure felt by the Pequot at this time. Unwilling to approach the Dutch, and probably unable to defeat the Narragansett, they hoped the powerful English could intercede and bring a favorable end to a simmering conflict that now clearly drained their power. It is clear from Governor Winthrop's own journal that the English understood some of the troubles the Pequot faced.[110]

In the end the Pequot and the Puritans came to an agreement of sorts. The English

---

[107] Cave, 59-60. Stone was regarded as an outcast in both English colonies. He had a reputation for unsavory practices and intemperate behavior inconsistent with accepted norms in either community.
[108] Cave, "Who Killed John Stone? A Note on the Origins of the Pequot War," 513.
[109] Ibid., 514.
[110] Ibid., 74-75; Bradford, 290-291.

agreed to conduct trade with the Pequot specifically, and the Pequot in turn offered land to encourage English settlement in the Connecticut River valley.[111] The motivation to lure the English into settlement in Connecticut seems clear enough today. It is likely that the Pequot hoped to have the English as an alternative trading partner to the Dutch, and a counterweight, perhaps, to the increasing pressures felt from competing tribes like the Narragansett.[112] The English demanded a high price for this and demanded more in wampum and pelts than the Pequot emissaries had brought with them. Additionally, the magistrates demanded that the Pequot deliver to them the participants in the killing of Captain Stone. The Pequot explained their version of events to the English and this seemed to satisfy the magistrates initially. However, the civic political leaders presented the Stone issue, and the Pequot explanations, to influential members of the clergy. The clergy, often the true source of influence in this theocracy, felt that it would be inadvisable to compromise with these unholy savages, regardless of how convincing their arguments.[113] So the English retained their provision for handing over the responsible parties to receive English justice.

There is some disagreement on the Pequot response to this demand. In any event, the English, perhaps without a full understanding of the Pequot response, concluded that the surviving participants would be delivered. We know from the letters and records which remain from the English side in this parley that the Puritan religious world-view overrode the initial impressions held by the magistrates. This overarching view prevailed

---

[111] Ibid., 69-71.
[112] Sylvester, 202-205.
[113] Cave, 75-76.

and continued to frame the future political dealings between the two peoples.[114]

By 1634 there were two well established English colonies on the New England coast. Plymouth was the older of the two but The Massachusetts Bay Colony had outpaced Plymouth in terms of growth. Massachusetts Bay Colony had maintained its Puritan character as it developed. Latecomers to the competition in south-central New England, the colony's leaders were generally cautious in its approach to developing settlements far from the coastline. Some tribes already recognized the Englishmen there as a source of influence in the contested markets along the Connecticut and Thames Rivers. In 1631 a delegation of Connecticut Indians had visited both Plymouth and Boston. The delegation's goal was to persuade the Englishmen to accept a tribute and establish a settlement in the valley. Such an arrangement would imply obligations to the tribes offering the land and tribute. Such a move would have very likely set the English in opposition or as a means to bypass the Pequot tribe. The English Governors Winthrop and Bradford suspected the intentions of the envoys and rejected the offer and its implied obligations.[115]

Despite some false starts and other obstacles, by 1634 the English had expanded further into Southern New England. Since 1631 some settlements had migrated away from the Puritan stronghold of Boston and Salem. Most notable was the colony established by an enthusiastic, non-conforming young minister, Roger Williams. His colony of Rhode Island was founded out of personal necessity rather than as a calculated means to expand English settlement in New England. Williams ran afoul of the

---

[114] Cave, "Who Killed John Stone? A Note on the Origins of the Pequot War," 516-517.
[115] Cave, 65.

authorities in Boston for his religious and political views and had fled to the south. He established good relations with the Wampanoag and Narragansett and chose their tribal lands to establish his colony.[116] Williams became an astute observer of the tribes and, more importantly, earned a measure of trust from the Indians he worked and lived with. His leverage with some of the tribes became a critical asset to the English as the crisis with the Pequots deepened.

---

[116] Henry William Elson, "Rhode Island and Providence Plantation," in *The History of the United States of America*, (Macmillan Company, New York, 1904) transcribed by Kathy Leigh, http://www.usahistory.info/New-England/Rhode-Island.html (accessed 10 November, 2007).

CHAPTER 3

WAR COMES TO CONNECTICUT

The English expansion into Connecticut during the years of 1634-35 brought the Puritans into sustained contact with the Pequot and their allies. English settlements meant an intensification of commerce and competition for resources. The closer proximity of the Indians and the English also denied the two communities a buffer that facilitated a sort of coexistence. This expansion of settlements would test the Puritan ability to coexist among the tribes of Southern New England and increase the risks of confrontation.

During the autumn and winter of 1634-35, colonists from the Massachusetts Bay began a more serious migration into the Connecticut. Puritan settlers uprooted themselves from the settlements of Newtown, Dorchester, and Watertown to seek more favorable land for settlement. Along the Connecticut River they established the settlements of Pyquag and Natianuck (today known as Wethersfield and Windsor respectively). Other English colonists migrated directly from the mother country. They voyaged, via Boston, to Connecticut where they laid claim to the land in the name of yet another commission from the mother country.[117] So in the space of only a few years time there were noticeably more Englishmen expanding the frontiers of their "New England".

As far as the two major European powers, The Netherlands and England, were concerned, Connecticut's status was still in dispute. However in the surge of settlement along the Connecticut River, the Dutch found themselves outflanked at their Hartford trading post by English traders and colonists. This effort strengthened the English

---

[117] Cave, 87-89.

position in the region relative to the Dutch. The English, despite their internal dissentions, now found themselves in a favorable position to contend with the Dutch for a stake in fur and wampum trade.

Both sides claimed the land but acted without urgency to resolve their dispute. In the background of this argument small bands of colonists from Massachusetts Bay, Plymouth colony, were establishing themselves in the region with confidence. The Dutch, meanwhile, continued with their practice of operating relatively small trading outposts in the region to represent their claims.

When pressed, the Dutch did assert their right to the region through reference to their past agreement with the Pequot. This claim was on shaky ground considering their violent falling out with the tribe and they did little else to enforce their claims. On a local level they attempted to intimidate the English, but failed to present a sufficiently persuasive threat.[118] The prospect of an armed conflict to decide this matter was not viewed as a realistic course of action for the Dutch since a favorable outcome to any such action was sufficiently in doubt.[119]

Direct settlement from the mother country was encouraged by Puritans still in England who also sought to make claims on the Connecticut land. English aristocrats planned to establish an independent colony at the mouth of the Connecticut River. They invested their trust in, John Winthrop Jr., the son of the Massachusetts governor, and

---

[118] William Bradford, *Of Plymouth Plantation, 1620-1647*, Samuel Eliot Morison, ed. (New York: Alfred A. Knopf Inc., 1970), 258-260.

[119] Alfred A. Cave, *The Pequot War* (Amherst, MA: University of Massachusetts Press, 1996), 83-84; Bradford, 260. To the north of the Dutch trading post, the House of Good Hope, the English from the Plymouth colony established a small trading outpost late in 1633. The Plymouth effort was strictly a commercial venture; they had no real need of the land only the access to commerce with the Indians While the Dutch were displeased by these developments and attempted to intimidate the English into abandoning their efforts they ultimately acquiesced to the presence of the Plymouth men.

commissioned him as executer of their designs and the colony's first governor.[120] In the autumn of 1635 this English expedition established themselves in a small fort at the mouth of the Connecticut River, naming it Fort Saybrook.[121] Leading the effort to construct the fort and the associated settlement was a Puritan from Scotland, Lion Gardiner. Gardiner owed his skill to experiences as a professional soldier and master of fortifications gained while serving in the Netherlands.[122]

---

[120] Cave, 90-91.
[121] Laurence M. Hauptman, "The Pequot War and Its Legacies," in *The Pequots in Southern New England, the Rise and Fall of an American Indian Nation,* Laurence M Hauptman, and James D Wherry, eds. (Norman and London: University of Oklahoma Press, 1990), 71.; Cave, 95.
[122] Cave, 91.; Lion Gardiner, *"So Must We Be One..., Otherwise We Shall Be All Gone Shortly,"* Narragansett Chief Miantonomi Tries to Form an Alliance Against Settlers in New England and Long Island, 1640s Collections of the Massachusetts Historical Society, third series, volume 3 (1833), 152–155.

The Pequot, adapting to the impact of expanding European contact and increased pressure from neighboring tribes struggled to navigate between their old norms and practices and the new political realities. Their traditional modes of cultivating relationships and alliances proved more difficult as European influence expanded. Political assumptions and calculations can only be guessed at since the Pequot did not leave records or detailed testimony addressing their situation. However, examination of the English records from 1634 and 1635 indicates that the Pequot did not understand the priorities and perspectives of the Puritans of the Massachusetts Bay Colony.

When the year 1635 came to a close the Pequot had still failed to deliver to the English the accused murderers of John Stone. Nor had they made any further effort to pay the tribute which included skins and four hundred fathoms of wampum.[123] Even a year after their agreement a Bay Colony trader, John Oldham inquired about these matters to the Pequot in the course of a trading expedition to the area. In reply he was informed that the Pequot elders had not approved of the agreement. It is fair to see the Pequot-Bay Colony agreement of 1634 as stillborn. The Pequot most likely believed that since Stone's death was a justified killing, they disagreed with any assertion that they should hand over their own people to English justice. Certainly this reply did nothing but to confirm the suspicions and biases of the English regarding the trustworthiness of their neighbors.

---

[123] Herbert Milton Sylvester, *Indian Wars of New England,* vol I (Boston: The Everett Press, 1910), 203-204.; Tara Prindle, Wampum History and Background, from http://www.nativetech.org/wampum/wamphist.htm,(accessed 26 November, 2007). A fathom (six feet of strung beads) of white wampum was worth ten shillings and double that for purple beads. A coat and *Buskins* "set thick with these Beads in pleasant wild works and a broad Belt of the same (Josselyn 1988: 101)" belonging to King Philip (Wampanoag) was valued at Twenty pounds. Even in the 1600s there was noted distinctiveness of Native-made wampum and the inability of others to counterfeit it, although attempts at imitations included beads of stone and other materials.

The tensions in the region were again inflamed when rumors began to circulate about the possibility of a Pequot effort to eliminate the English settlements in Connecticut. These rumors have been captured in English accounts from the period, but the initial source of these reports is difficult to discern. By most accounts the reports came from competing tribes who may have been seeking to further bias the Europeans against the Pequot.[124] While there may have been some substance to the report it seems unlikely that such a notion was seriously entertained. Any gain achieved by the expulsion of the English would be offset by the risks of war on an already stressed population. Perhaps the Pequot could revive their trade agreements with the Dutch, but that was a questionable proposition.

Tension with the Dutch and uncertainty about Pequot intentions heightened the perception of risk involved the expansion into Connecticut. Nevertheless, it seems that one of the dominant concerns for the leaders in Bay Colony was the potential that the transplants would drift away from the tight embrace of both the church and the colonial government. It was with some reluctance that Governor Winthrop granted "permission" to relocate to the region.[125] It appears that in their consideration of the emigration to Connecticut, the Puritans of the Bay Colony were inwardly focused. There seems to have been little reflection about the impact this expansion would have on the other associated parties whose paths and purposes would intersect in this endeavor.

Small English settlements were established with every intention that they would grow and prosper. Each English settlement established drew in the trade from

---

[124] Cave, 98.; Bradford, 294.
[125] Cave, 95-96.

surrounding tribes and naturally intensified the competition for access and resources. A successful trading outpost supported the development and expansion of English farms and villages.[126] Ownership in these settlements was considered a long term prospect with the expectation of expansion. So, barring a catastrophic pestilence or war, it was all but certain that the European population would increase; this was particularly true if there were financial incentives to support greater migration. In this game it was inevitable that the native people would begin to feel pressured to further compromise with the newcomers or to eject them.

The Murder of John Oldham

In such a charged setting it seems inevitable that there would be some other provocation to inflame the existing suspicions of the Europeans or the native tribes. That provocation came with the murder of a Massachusetts Bay trader named John Oldham. Oldham had first ventured into the region in 1633 on an overland exploration to assess the value of trade with the tribes living there.[127] His contact with the natives was favorable enough, but not sufficiently productive to elicit much enthusiasm at the time from the leaders in Boston. After the Pequot journey to Boston in 1634 the door seemed open for more productive trading. His later trips to the region were by sea and sufficiently profitable to encourage further voyages.

It was in the course of one of these trading missions that Oldham and his two sons

---

[126] William Cronon. *Changes in the Land: Indians, Colonists, and the Ecology of New England* (New York: Hill and Wang, 1983), 98-99.
[127] Richard Radune, *Pequot Plantation-The Story of an Early Colonial Settlement* (Branford, Connecticut: Research in Time Publications, 2005), 19-20.

were overcome and killed just off the shore from Block Island. Oldham's small boat was discovered by a trailing ship piloted by John Gallop, another Boston trader sailing to southern New England.

According to Gallop's testimony, when they encountered Oldham's boat there were still Indians aboard. He recognized quickly that something was wrong, and to confirm his suspicions the anchor was pulled the occupants attempted to flee in the boat as Gallop approached. Some of the Indians fled toward shore, in a canoe, and others presumably attempted to swim. Gallop gave chase to Oldham's boat, overtook it, and he and his small crew overcame the remaining boarders after a brief skirmish. The first man to surrender to Gallop was bound and taken aboard his boat. The next was not so fortunate. Fearing that two on his ship would place him in danger, Gallop instead threw the bound man overboard. On searching Oldham's ship they found his mutilated body but no sign of his sons or two Narragansett guides. Gallop decided to sail for Fort Saybrook to report what had occurred. Following this, he departed for Boston to bring news of the event.[128] At the time of the incident it was not clear who was responsible for the murders.

The prisoner Gallop brought back with him confessed that the murders were actually a plot by some Narragansetts and their allies. Undoubtedly there was some difficulty in piecing together the motivation for this crime. In Winthrop's account of the event it appears that the murders were the result of some inner turmoil with the Narragansett tribe.[129]

There is still some confusion about which tribe actually participated in the

---

[128] John, Winthrop, *The History of New England From 1630 to 1649*, vol. I, James Kendal Hosmer, ed. (New York: Schribner and Sons, 1908), 183-184.; Radune, 16-18.
[129] Winthrop, 184.

murders. Most evidence points to Block Island Indians, a small band, tied to the Narragansett through alliances with the eastern Niantic. Interestingly enough, the two Narragansett who were with Oldham were not killed but did in fact make it to land. They informed their sachems, Canonicus and Miantonomi about the murders. Clearly, these two sachems recognized the danger this put their tribes in and they enlisted the help of their English neighbor, Roger Williams, in the crafting of a letter expressing their regret over the nasty incident.[130] They sent this letter with emissaries, the two Narragansetts, hired by Oldham as guides, to Boston with their assurances that they would take action against these outlaws. So, in the standard cycle of revenge killings, it seems that the Narragansett were saying that they would take action on behalf of the English to avenge this crime though there is little evidence any such an action occurred.

Interestingly the Indian captive identified the two emissaries as being complicit in the plot to murder Oldham. While this shocked and angered the new Massachusetts governor, Henry Vane, he decided to respect their role as emissaries of the Narragansett sachems and not detain them on the spot.[131] The captive did provide the magistrates with some good news, when he informed them that the two boys accompanying Oldham had not been killed but were captives. John Winthrop related some of the English findings, "But, upon examination of the Indian who was brought prisoner to us, we found that all the sachems of the Naragansett, except Canonicus and Miantunnomoh, were contrivers of Mr. Oldham's Death; and the occasion was, because he went to make peace, and trade

---

[130] Ibid.
[131] Cave, 105-106.

with the Pekods [sic] last year, as is before related."[132] So when pressed for reasons behind the Oldham murder the justification given was Oldham's trading with the Pequot. If that was indeed the case then the Narragansett motive could be the same motive that drove the Pequot to murder Indians trading at the Dutch outpost at Hartford. As the Pequots had demonstrated in 1633 with their attacks against Indians who sought to trade directly with the Dutch, the Indians were not above using violent actions to intimidate and isolate their opposition from the Europeans.[133] Interestingly enough, the report we have from John Winthrop's journal portrayed John Oldham's spring voyage to trade with the Pequot as less than successful.[134]

Initially in this event the English seemed to calculate their response quite carefully. Governor Vane sent the envoys back to their sachem and dispatched a message to be delivered through Roger Williams. In this he communicated that the English expected the return of all captives and further, any participants in the attack should be delivered up for investigation. The Narragansett sachems complied with part of the demand, returning the two English boys, and some of Oldham's goods. When queried as to why they could not deliver any participants to the English, the Narragansett were evasive. The sachem Miantonomi told the English that the guilty parties had sought shelter among the Pequots.[135] This information, tied with the gestures of goodwill inherent in the return of the captives and some of Oldham's goods, succeeded in

---

[132] Winthrop, 184.; Francis Jennings offers another explanation for the Narragansett actions in his work the *Invasion of America*, 206-208. There is some thought that perhaps Oldham was held responsible for the smallpox epidemic of 1633-34.
[133] Cave, 58.
[134] Alden T. Vaughan, *"Pequots and Puritans: The Causes of the War of 1637,"* in *The American Indian: Past and Present,* Roger L. Nichols and George R. Adams, eds. (New York: John Wiley and Sons, Inc., 1971), 64.
[135] Cave, 106-108.

deflecting some of the English wrath.

There is no real evidence that the guilty parties ever sought shelter among the Pequots at all. While it was entirely possible, the fact that even the two Narragansett emissaries were never returned to the English raises doubt. The back and forth messages and conflicting stories must have taxed the ability of the Puritan leaders to discern the truth. For the Puritans, who imagined themselves to be actors in a greater spiritual struggle of good versus evil, the political maneuvering from the tribal leaders and the perception of evasiveness reinforced the view that the natives could be dealt with but not fully trusted. In one regard this incident and its aftermath served to reinforce the deeply ingrained suspicions the English held concerning the Indians.[136] More importantly perhaps, incidents like the murders of Stone and Oldham surely heightened the sense of peril some English may have felt about their position in New England.

An English War Party;
"And Thus Began the War between the Indians and Us in these Parts"[137]

Rather than wait to see if the tribal leaders would fulfill the demands of the government in Boston the English decided to look after the matter themselves. An expedition was arranged under the leadership of a Boston magistrate, John Endecott, who commanded the Boston Militia company. In all some ninety men were involved.[138] The target for the English wrath was initially the settlements on Block Island. Captain Endecott was instructed to accomplish four tasks on his expedition. The first was to

---

[136] Karen Ordahl Kupperman, *English Perceptions of Treachery, 1583-1640: The Case of the American 'Savages',*" *The Historical Journal.* 20, no. 2 (June 1977), 278.

[137] Lion Gardiner, "*Relation of the Pequot Warres,*" (Hartford: Hartford Press, 1901), 12.

[138] Winthrop, 186.

conduct a raid against the Block Island tribe and. More specifically "They had commission to put to death the men of Block Island."[139] The following two tasks related to the first. Endecott was to take as captives the women and children found on the island, "…and to take possession of the Island".[140] His last task was clearly a bridge to the other festering concern of the Bay Colony's leaders. It would be the most fateful for the Pequot. Endecott was to proceed on to the land of the Pequots and deliver the English demand that the tribe hand over the killers of Stone, in addition to the large payment of wampum.[141] Furthermore, if the Pequots refused to meet the English demands, the Puritan leadership instructed Endecott that the taking of Pequot children as hostages was allowable. This was a technique of coercion similarly used by John Smith in the Virginia colony.[142] At the time however, the goals, and most probably the methods, of the expedition were explicitly condoned by the Colony's influential religious leaders.

Alfred Cave provides a good glimpse into the nature of the man tasked to lead this heavy-handed expedition. He is described as "ill-suited for the task of negotiating with the Pequot, being by nature of impatient and sometimes violent temperament."[143] Endecott was not so much sent, as unleashed, on the Block Islanders and Pequot. Undoubtedly, he shared the belief prevalent among many of the Puritans, that the natives were heathen, deceitful, and moreover, dangerous. The murders of Stone and Oldham seemed to confirm this. The Puritan leaders in Boston clearly felt that a strong message had to be sent and any nascent threats extinguished: the Englishmen were to be feared

---

[139] Ibid.
[140] Ibid.
[141] Radune, 24.
[142] Kupperman, 267.
[143] Cave, 109.

and dealt with honorably.

On August 22, 1636 the company departed Boston to land what can be considered the opening blow in the Pequot War. The ninety soldiers and two guides sailed south to Block Island in three small pinnaces. The raid was not a surprise. The English were received by a war-party of over fifty men. Once of Endecott's subordinates, Captain John Underhill, relates that they were met at the beach with a flurry of arrows. The initial skirmish lacked intensity and although it disrupted the English landing, the English remained determined.[144] Once ashore they established a camp for the night and prepared themselves for the next day's action.

The next morning the English party moved further into the island, searching for the Block Island settlements. They were successful in locating two sizable settlements complete with large fields of corn, but in both cases the villages were deserted. By the end of the first day Endecott's party had determined that their quarry had sought shelter in some of the swamps on the Island.[145] In the spirit of their orders they occupied themselves with torching the crops and the villages belonging to the tribe. Encounters with the natives were limited to fleeting glimpses and brief, shadowy engagements. While the English had thus far suffered no significant casualties in the action, they had not fully accomplished the grim task they had been given. However Underhill sums up the feeling at that point, "The Indians playing least in sight, wee spent our time, and could no more advantage our selves then wee had already done, having slaine [sic]some

---

[144] Underhill, John, "*Newes from America; Or, A New and Experimentall Discoverie of New England; Containing, A Trve Relation of Their War-like Proceedings These Two Yeares Last Past, with a Figure of the Indian Fort, or Palizado,*" Paul Royster ed., Digital Commons At UNL, www.digitalcommons.unl.edu/etas/37/ (accessed October 24, 2007), 4.
[145] Ibid., 6-7.

fourteen, & maimed others, wee imbarqued [sic]our selves, and set saile [sic]for *Seasbrooke* fort.".". It is certain, however, that with the burning of the villages and the destruction of their crops and any visible stores, that the Block Islanders would be hard pressed in the coming fall and winter. So at the close of the second day Endecott re-embarked his small force and sailed for Connecticut.[146]

The Connecticut settlement had not been privy to the decisions made by the men in Boston. Once they learned of the action, and Endecott's charge, they quickly estimated the potential impacts. At Fort Saybrook the garrison's commander, Lion Gardiner, feared for his small settlement if the Boston men stirred up the wrath of the Pequots through their heavy demands:

> And suddenly after came Capt. Endecott, Capt. Turner, and Capt. Undrill [sic][Underhill], with a company of soldiers, well fitted, to Seabrook and made that place their rendezvous or seat of war, and that to my great grief, for, said I, you come hither to raise these wasps about my ears, and then you will take wing and flee away; but when I had seen their commission I wondered, and made many allegations against the manner of it, but go they did to Pequit [sic], and as they came without acquainting any of us in the River with it, so they went against our will, for I knew that I should lose our corn-field;[147]

It is fair to say from this account that Gardiner was not convinced at all that the Pequots would be fearful of English power or immediately acquiesce to their demands. Gardiner understood that the Boston men were intent on delivering their ultimatum and feared for the survival of his garrison. Yet he urged an action which could only have further aggravated the situation:

> Sirs, Seeing you will go, I pray you, if you don't load your Barks with

---
[146] Ibid.
[147] Gardiner, 9.

> Pequits [sic], load them with corn, for that is now gathered with them, and dry, ready to put into their barns, and both you and we have need of it, and I will send my shallop and hire this Dutchman's boat, there present, to go with you, and if you cannot attain your end of the Pequits, yet you may load your barks with corn, which will be welcome to Boston and to me,…[148]

So Gardiner proposed the theft of some of the Pequot harvest if things did not go as Endecott anticipated. His plan was accepted and the party eventually departed to contact the Pequot along the Pequot River (Thames River, Connecticut today), which was a short journey to the east from Fort Saybrook. The English entered the mouth of the river and were hailed from the riverbanks by the Pequot and their western Niantic allies. The English were silent and stern as they watched the Pequots on the shore. Endecott's party spent the night aboard their ships, watched by the Indians who by now had grown wary about the intentions of the Englishmen.[149] In the morning the Pequot sent an emissary out to the boats to confer with the English. There Endecott presented the demands as charged in Boston; Stone's and Oldham's murderers and one thousand fathoms, or roughly eighteen hundred meters, of wampum.[150]

If they could not deliver on these demands, then Endecott informed the emissary that they would take twenty children as hostages. It is hard to imagine that this would be an acceptable situation to any tribe, let alone a tribe which was still a power to be reckoned with in southeastern New England. Obviously there is no record of the Pequot perspective on such a demand. There is some thought that perhaps the English were merely fulfilling some sense of obligation by presenting the Pequot with demands, a

---

[148] Ibid.
[149] Underhill, 8.
[150] Radune, 26.; Winthrop, 186.

pretense of negotiation. This seems to find some grounding in Underhill's account: "They not thinking we intended warre [sic] went on cheerefully untill [sic] they come to Pequeat [sic] river."[151]

At this point it may be useful to recall some critical issues which must have immediately played out for the Pequot. First, the tribe had just suffered through the devastating epidemic of 1633-34. The demand for hostages at any time was bound to be a detestable burden, even more so under these circumstances. Then the demand for tribute in the form of wampum was appropriate for a subordinate or subjugated tribe, but not a sovereign people. Finally, the demand for those associated with the Stone murders in addition to the payment and the hostages must have made clear to the Pequot the English view of their status. Obviously the English viewed them as a subordinate entity. To a proud people this must have been an unacceptable affront. Only the naiveté born of arrogance could assume submission of this combination of demands. The English either meant war from the start or naively assumed that the righteous intervention of God would soften the hearts of the heathen.

In response to these demands the Pequot elder explained again to the English the circumstances surrounding Stone's death.[152] One of his primary claims was that the murderers had no idea that Stone was English, as opposed to Dutch. His explanations

---

[151] Underhill, 8-9.
[152] Underhill, 10-12.; Cave makes note of Underhill's explanation but incorrectly concludes that the "prince" mentioned is Sassacus. Cave then goes on to imply that Sassacus was himself involved in the murder. In fact it seems that the Pequot envoy began his parley by explaining the murder of the sachem Tatobem. but we saw there was no remedy, their expectation must be granted, or else they would not send him ashore, which they promised they would doe, if wee would answer their desires : wee [sic] sent them so much aboord [sic] according to demand, and they according to their promise sent him ashore, but first slew him, this, much exasperated our spirits, and made us vow a revenge;"

were poorly received by the impatient Endecott. The English countered the Pequot assertion that they could not distinguish the Dutch from English and if the Pequot would not satisfy English demands then there would be a fight.[153] Finally the emissary was allowed to return to shore to discuss the English terms with some of the assembled tribal leaders. Gardiner, another witness to the negotiations, relayed a brief description:

> …and demanded the Pequit [sic] Sachem to come into parley. But it was returned for answer, that he was from home, 'but within three hours he would come; and so from three to six, and thence to nine, there came none. But the Indians came without arms to our men, in great numbers, and they talked with my men, whom they knew; but in the end, at a word given, they all on a sudden ran away from our men, as they stood in rank and file, and not an Indian more was to be seen: and all this while before, they carried all their stuff away, and thus was that great parley ended.[154]

In a rapid escalation Endecott moved some of his men ashore and assembled them on high ground nearby in anticipation of violence. Again they conferred with the Pequot emissary who now informed them that their grand sachem, Sassacus, was in fact on Long Island visiting a tributary tribe there.[155] The English held their ground and waited. Accounts from John Underhill describe the English militia, waiting in full armor, on a warm September afternoon for the emissary to locate some person of authority with whom to discuss the matter further. It is fair to surmise that the longer they waited the less agreeable the already stern Englishmen would become. Finally, what limited patience Endecott had was evaporated. Fearing that the delay was giving the enemy time to develop a plan against his force, he gave instructions to his company and they moved

---

[153] Ibid, 11.
[154] Gardiner, 127.
[155] Underhill, 12.; Cave, 116.

forward toward the mass of Pequots. Underhill noted that at this time they saw only men among the natives, no women or children seemed to be present. Fearing that a fight was imminent the English were determined to strike the first blow.[156]

The English attack was at first met with no notable resistance. They entered the village and set fire to the dwellings and provisions, and some of Gardiner's men attempted to gather as much corn from the field as they could. So the war against the Pequot opened with this inconclusive raid. Much like the punitive raid against the Block Islanders, it seemed as if the English did very little, if any, actual killing but their destructiveness undoubtedly opened the door for reprisal, which is exactly what occurred.[157]

As he feared, Gardiner and his men were the targets of the first Pequot counterattack. To his evident dismay, Endecott and his company boarded their boats and set sail to return to Fort Saybrook while Gardiner and his men were still ashore. "But they all set sail, and my men were pursued by the Indians, and they hurt some of the Indians, and two of them came home wounded."[158] The Bay Colony men returned to Boston, leaving the Connecticut colonists to fend for themselves over the winter as they faced an enraged and embattled Pequot nation.

---

[156] Ibid., 12-13.
[157] Cave, 116-117.; Winthrop, 189.
[158] Gardiner, 127.

In Boston the Puritan leaders received irritated communications from Lion Gardiner as well as the governor of the Plymouth Colony. In their view, Boston had taken a reckless action which exposed their settlements, not the Bay Colony, to assault and destruction. The Puritan leaders in Boston had a different view of the issue. Winthrop's journal entries indicate that the leaders in Boston assumed the issue settled for the time being.[159] The leaders in Boston appeared smug in their view that they could chastise the Pequots for their intransigence, like criminals or pirates. Gardiner and other Connecticut colonists assessed that the Pequot would make no careful distinction when meting out their retribution. There is no evidence to support the idea that the Boston colony truly

---

[159] Winthrop, 194.

anticipated the response they would soon get from the Pequot. This shortsightedness reflected a lack of awareness and careful thought on the matter at hand. It would be hard to imagine such a rash action taken if the issue involved another European nation's settlement(s). The Puritans in Boston saw their expedition as a punitive expedition to bring righteous justice to a malicious people.[160]

In Connecticut Sassacus' warriors sought revenge against the English for the violence of September. While the Puritan leaders in Boston sat out the winter, a hit and run conflict between the vengeful Pequot and the colonists was simmering. The Pequot raiders killed any English caught along the river or in the woods outside of the settlements, if they were fortunate. If they were captured they faced almost certain torture at the hands of their captors before they died.[161] At Fort Saybrook, the Pequot isolated the garrison and ambushed foraging parties if they strayed from the protection of the Fort. Again, Gardiner's narrative gives us a glimpse of the dangers faced by the English along the Connecticut River in the wake of Endecott's raid. Here his account involves a small party sent from the Fort to gather food:

> …Now these men not regarding the charge I had given them, three of them went a mile from the house a fowling; and having loaded themselves with fowl they returned. But the Pequits [sic] let them pass first, till they had loaded themselves, but at their return they arose out of their ambush, and shot them all three; one of them escaped through the corn, shot through the leg, the other two they tormented. Then the next day I sent the shallop to fetch the five men, and the rest of the corn that was broken down, and they found but three, as is above said, and when they had gotten that they left the rest; and as soon as they were gone a little way from shore, they saw the house on fire.[162]

---

[160] Underhill, 1.; Winthrop, 186.
[161] Gardiner, 11-12.
[162] Ibid.

The garrison requested assistance and some of the plantations within Connecticut responded by sending a force of militia to augment the Fort. Later they were relieved by a smaller, but heavily armed force sent from Boston.[163]

Throughout the winter and into the spring the Pequot's anger was unabated. On April 23, 1637 between one and two hundred Pequot warriors participated in a raid on the English settlement at Wethersfield, south of Hartford. To the English in the settlement the attack must have seemed a grim fulfillment of the stories of savagery which they had undoubtedly heard. Nine English were killed in the attack, including a woman and child, and two young female captives were carried off by the attackers.[164] In balance, it is fair to say that the Indian attack did less grievous damage to the community as a whole than did Endecott's expedition on the Pequot river the previous autumn. Rumors of other such raids spread along the river, although most of those were later proven false. In the winter and spring of 1637 such rumors held their own power.

So by the spring of 1637 the Puritan leaders in Boston were facing what they had probably hoped to avoid all along. Their heavy-handed demands and punitive expedition had effectively turned what was a matter of criminal activity, perhaps piracy, into a war between two contending societies.

At some point soon after Endecott's raid along the Pequot River, Sassacus and his followers realized that their greatest danger was now the English. If before they were uncertain about their relations with the Europeans, they now must have understood that there would be a bloodletting before relations could be resumed with the English, if they

---

[163] Underhill, 14-15.
[164] Vaughan, 66.

could at all. In this context the Pequot understood that their greatest chance for success was to ally themselves with the other powerful tribes in the area, chiefly the Narragansett.[165] Such an alliance would accomplish two things; first it would neutralize the enemy at their doorstep, and second it would present the English with a broader challenge of contending with the two major tribes and their subordinate allies. Unfortunately for the Pequot, they were too late in this realization.

As far back as the summer of 1636 word reached the English from the mouth of Uncas, the sachem of the Mohegans, that the Pequot were plotting against English traders and settlements along the Connecticut River valley.[166] These native rivals to the Pequots found eager listeners among many of the English. Accounts of English traders, saved literally by the wind of divine intervention from the clutches of the treacherous Pequots, made their way back to the English leaders in Boston and Plymouth. English unease increased when the Pequot failed to deliver fully on the demands made by the English following the death of Captain Stone.[167] So as the likelihood of continued hostilities with the Pequot became more apparent the Puritan leaders in Boston ironically began to rely on Rhode Island Plantation governor, Roger Williams, for an assessment of Indian intentions.[168]

It was probably from Roger Williams that the English in Boston learned of the attempted alliance between the Pequot and the Narragansett. Naturally Boston urged

---

[165] Bradford, 294-295.
[166] Cave, 98-99; Winthrop, 190. There was an ongoing concern that the two dominant tribes in the region would strike a bargain and turn on the English. In one case Roger Williams wrote to Winthrop warning him of this possibility and in another case Jonathan Brewster, a Plymouth man, wrote to Winthrop to relay the rumors of a Pequot plot.
[167] Cave, 98-100.
[168] Sylvester, Herbert Milton, *Indian Wars of New England, Vol I,* Boston: The Everett Press, 1910,. 231.

Williams to intervene and prevent such an alliance if he could. This was eventually accomplished through a series of negotiations conducted directly with the leadership of the Narragansett tribe. The treaty approved in October 1636 stipulated that neither group, the English nor Narragansett, would make a separate peace with the Pequot.[169] This completed the isolation of the Pequot and their Western Niantic allies.

The Pequot were emboldened by their successes along the river, sailing at one point within range of Fort Saybrook to challenge and taunt the English. They ridiculed the defenders and their Christian God. It is, however, not out of character for the style of warfare to which the Indians were accustomed. In their ritualistic combat it was not uncommon for opponents to taunt one another. Taunts and insults mentioning their religion only inflamed anger of the Englishmen.[170]

In response to the attacks along the river in Connecticut, the civic leaders assembled to determine a response to the Pequot. In May 1637 they declared that they would wage an offensive campaign against the Pequot. The local courts authorized the conscription of a militia of ninety men to execute this war. Command of this force fell to Captain John Mason, a thirty-seven year old professional soldier who had served in the Netherlands with an English expeditionary army before his emigration. Mason's force was assembled and provisioned for the campaign. They were encouraged by their clergy

---

[169] Radune, 27.; Winthrop, 193-194.

[170] Cave, 136; Underhill, 14. Following Endicott's initial raid the Pequot targeted the Saybrook fort. In one instance after an inconclusive skirmish the Pequot approached the fort wearing captured English clothes and boldly taunted the English inside, "..we have one amongst us that if he could kill but one of you more, he would be equall [sic] with God, and as the *English* mans God is, so would hee[sic] be; this blasphemous speech troubled the hearts of the souldiers [sic], but they knew not how to remedy it in respect of their weaknesse.[sic]"

who, in the account relayed by Captain Edward Johnson, encouraged them with exhortations and scriptural references to, "execute vengeance upon the heathen and correction among their people…" and to "…make their multitudes fall under your warlike weapons…"[171] These were not words to inspire charitable moderation in the listeners; these were words to incite terrible vengeance, which is exactly what happened.

The authorities in Massachusetts made ready to dispatch another force to continue the prosecution of the war against the Pequot. As the civic leaders in the Bay colony levied their force for the expedition they attempted to enlist the aid of their neighbors in the Plymouth Colony.

In his book on the Pequot War, Cave highlights in some detail the existing tensions between the Plymouth and Massachusetts Bay Colonies. These tensions all contributed to the reluctance, verging on outright refusal, of the Plymouth Colony to participate in this conflict. Perhaps the overarching reason for Governor Winslow's resistance to the idea was the failure of the Puritan leaders to appraise the Plymouth leaders of the intentions behind Endecott's mission. The Plymouth governor raised secondary objections in a tit-for-tat exchange with the Bay Colony men. In reply, the leaders in Boston attempted to persuade the Plymouth men that the cause was worthy, and that if the English failed to show a strong front and defeat the Pequot threat, then other Indians would be emboldened and the English position in New England would be jeopardized.[172] This view carries less weight today given the separation of time, our current assessments of population size, and the broader understanding of the strategic

---

[171] Edward, Johnson, *Wonder-Working Providence of Sions Savior in New England*, J. Franklin Jameson, ed. (New York, Charles Schribner and Sons, 1910),165-166.; Cave, 137.
[172] Winthrop, 213-214.

situation faced by the English colonies. At the time however, given the Puritan worldview of a harsh, untamed land inhabited by treacherous heathen, and the reality of increased competition with other European states staking their own claims in North America, such a concern can be more fully understood.

The appeal from Boston to Plymouth for support eventually earned them a grudging pledge of fifty soldiers and a crew for a small boat. The soldiers never saw action in the fight, which ended before they were dispatched. In this way Plymouth made a gesture of support for their brothers to the north, but it was nothing more than a gesture, and they elected to take no part in the war.[173]

The gathering English forces from Boston and Connecticut sought and received aid from their Indian allies for this campaign. After some negotiation at Fort Saybrook, the Mohegan sachems' pledge of warriors to help fight the Pequot was accepted. While this increased the size of the force Mason had available, it was still far smaller than the numbers available to the Pequot. While still at Saybrook the commanders- Mason, Underhill, and Gardiner wrestled with the development of a sound course of action for their operation.

There was little solid information for the English to consider as they planned. Mason had been instructed by the Connecticut magistrates to land in the Pequot River and carry out his operation. While this was a more direct route it presented some significant risks to the English force. The English were relatively few in number and they were not familiar with the terrain.[174] They had Mohegan allies, but Uncas's force was

---

[173] Cave, 139.
[174] Cave, 144.

also quite small and of unknown quality. Mason and his subordinates realized that they may be able to preserve some measure of surprise if they moved by sea to Narragansett Bay and marched overland from the East. This course of action would also provide them the opportunity to recruit the Narragansett for this effort. There was still some disagreement on the issue, so Mason sought the counsel of the clergy to determine the best course of action in their attack on the Pequots. After a night of reflection the chaplain gave his feedback. Mason and his fellow officers elected to begin their campaign from Narragansett Bay rather than a direct approach through Pequot harbor[175] based on the advice of the chaplain. On Friday, May 19th the English force departed Saybrook by boat to begin the decisive campaign of the conflict.

Wrapped in Flames: The Defeat of the Pequot

On Saturday the 20th the Connecticut men under Mason arrived in Narragansett Bay. They stayed afloat for the Sabbath and a storm prevented their landing on Monday. Finally on Tuesday the 23rd, they landed and marched to meet the Narragansett sachem Miantonomi to secure passage through Narragansett territory. Miantonomi agreed to the English passage but did not initially commit forces to the venture. Mason was anxious to move against the Pequot before they could determine the location and size of his force.[176] On Wednesday the 24th Mason's force, composed of ninety English and seventy Mohegan, began an overland march to the west to enter Pequot territory and eliminate the seat of Pequot power, the fortified villages at Mystic and Weinshauks.[177] In the course of

---

[175] Ibid.,144-145.
[176] Sylvester,260-263.
[177] Cave, 143-145.

their two day march the force absorbed a force of approximately 500 Narragansett warriors. Many of the Narragansett drifted off the further the force penetrated into Pequot territory; however, the Mohegan force remained with the militia.[178] Mason received information that an additional English force from Boston had arrived and was following, yet he decided not to wait. His concern at this point was detection by the Pequot, which would, at the least, cause his quarry to flee. At the worst it could open his small force to ambush in the heart of the Sassacus' territory. Mason and his captains determined that Mystic was the easier of the two villages to reach and attack quickly. This force of 300-400 soldiers and Indian braves approached to within two miles of the fortified village before halting.[179]

In this case the decision to approach from the east was a sound one. The English set out to execute their assault on the village at about one in the morning on the 26th of May. Their Mohegan and Narragansett allies guided the English into position. Mason's plan was to divide his force, surround the village, and begin his assault. There was no consideration at this point to any further parley with the Pequot. This would be an attack to overcome the defenses and crush any resistance. Captain Underhill, leading one portion of the English force, gives us his account:

> Captain John Mason, approaching to the west end, where it had an entrance to pass into it; myself marching to the south side, surrounding the fort, placing the Indians, for we had about three hundred of them, without side of our soldiers in a ring battalia [sic], giving a volley of shot upon the

---

[178] Radune, 33.
[179] John Underhill, "Captain John Underhill Justifies the Attack on Mystic Village in the Pequot War (1637) 1638," in *Major Problems in American Military History,* John W Chambers II and G.Kurt Piehler, eds. (Boston and New York: Houghton Mifflin Company, 1999), 40-41.; Cave,147; the Boston force went on to raid some Pequot cornfields planted on Block Island. They suffered no known casualties.

> fort. So remarkable it appeared to us, that we could not but admire at the providence of God in it that soldiers so unexpert [sic] in the use of their arms, should give so complete a volley, as though the finger of God had touched both match and flint. Which volley being given at break of day, and themselves fast asleep for the most part, bred in them such a terror, that they brake forth in a most doleful cry; so as if God had not fitted the hearts of men for service, it would have bred in them a commiseration towards them. But every man being bereaved of pity, fell upon the work without compassion, considering the blood they shed of our native countrymen, and how barbarously they had dealt with them, and slain, first and last, about thirty persons.[180]

Following their initial volleys there was little response from the village. The English were resolved to close and finish their attack. At this point the story becomes somewhat confused, as nearly any account of combat at close quarters tends to be.

What can be accurately determined is that the English entered the village where they intended to fight at close quarters with their enemy. The Indian allies maintained (for the most part) the ring around the village. Examining the accounts of both Mason and Underhill we can see that the Pequot often waited until the Englishmen were close in among the wigwams before they engaged them with whatever weapons they had at hand. Underhill again gives us a good account of the close fighting and the toll it began to take on the small English force:

> Captain Mason and myself entering into the wigwams, he was shot, and received many arrows against his headpiece. God preserved him from many wounds. Myself received a shot in the left hip, through a sufficient buff coat, that if I had not been supplied with such a garment, the arrow would have pierced through me. Another I had received in between the neck and the shoulders, hanging in the linen of my headpiece. Others of our soldiers were shot, some through the shoulders, some through the face, some in the head, some in the legs, Captain Mason and myself losing each of us a man, and had near twenty wounded.[181]

---

[180] John Underhill, "Captain John Underhill Justifies the Attack on Mystic Village in the Pequot War (1637) 1638," 41.

[181] Underhill, 42-43.

There should be no doubt that once the battle was joined inside the walled village the confusion must have been tremendous. The English matchlocks were of limited utility at close quarters, so after an initial volley most killing was accomplished with swords, daggers, and the pistols which some officers carried. "having our swords in our right hand, our Carbins [sic] or Muskets in our left hand, we approached the Fort."[182] Mason's account communicates some of the confusion of the fight as the English operated in small bands within the walls of the fortified village, fighting Pequot in and among their dwellings. It was in the midst of this fight that Mason decided to set fire to the wood and bark structures and burn the Indians out.[183] Underhill describes the scene:

> Captaine [sic] *Mason* and my selfe losing each of us a man, and had neere [sic] twentie [sic] wounded: most couragiously [sic] these *Pequeats* behaved themselves: but seeing the Fort was to hotte [sic] for us, wee devised a way how wee might save our selves and prejudice them, Captaine [sic] *Mason* entering into a Wigwam, brought out a fire-brand, after hee had wounded many in the house, then hee set fire on the West-side where he entred, my selfe [sic] set fire on the South end with a traine [sic]of Powder, the fires of both meeting in the center of the Fort blazed most terribly, and burnt all in the space of halfe an houre [sic]; many couragious fellowes [sic] were unwilling to come out, and fought most desperately through the Palisadoes,..."[184]

With the spread of the fire within the village the English withdrew. Outside of the village they resumed their cordon with some of the Indian allies. Fleeing Pequots were often shot or cut down. Within the space of a half hour the fire had consumed the village and killed any who remained in it. Estimates for the numbers killed and wounded vary greatly.

---

[182] Underhill, 34.

[183] John, Mason, *A Brief History of the Pequot War: Especially of the Memorable Taking of their Fort at Mistick in Connecticut in 1637,* in *Major Problems in American Military History,* John W Chambers II and G.Kurt Piehler, eds. (Boston and New York: Houghton Mifflin Company, 1999), 43.

[184] Underhill, *News from America*, 34-35.

Underhill asserts that the Pequot themselves count 400 dead.[185] Mason, on the other hand, estimated between "the Number of six or seven Hundred, as some of themselves confessed." Captain Mason viewed the outcome of the fight in a manner consistent with the view of divine justification for the actions against the Pequot. "…the just Judgment of GOD…"[186] The English for their part suffered two killed and twenty wounded. This was the European way of war brought to bear against the native people.

The Indian allies who had remained with the Mason's force experienced mixed reactions. It can be fair to surmise that they had never seen war made with the same ferocity and scale that they had witnessed that day. Although the accompanying Indian warriors could admire some of the courage displayed in the English storming of the fortified village they were at the same time repulsed by the terrible bloodletting which did not seem to discriminate between men, women, or children.[187]

This was not the end to the fighting, but it was a decisive act. With a good proportion of his force weary and wounded from the two days of marching, Mason prudently decided against another assault on the Sassacus's fortified village, Weinshauks.[188] His company departed and marched toward Pequot harbor to meet their ships. Along the way they were engaged by some warriors drawn from nearby settlements. In a series of skirmishes they inflicted further casualties on the Pequot. At this point Mason's force was potentially at risk. His Narragansett allies were drifting away in significant numbers. Underhill and Mason both record their scorn for this

---

[185] Underhill, 35.
[186] Ibid.
[187] Ibid, 42-43.
[188] Cave, 152.

behavior from the Narragansett. The English and their remaining Indian allies prudently made haste to withdraw from contact.[189] Upon reaching the bay, Mason's had his wounded placed aboard their ships and sent back toward Fort Saybrook. Mason and his remaining force continued overland, to Saybrook. The Pequot broke off their half-hearted pursuit.

In the Pequot war council at Weinshauks, the leadership deliberated over what further action to take. By some accounts Sassacus hoped to strike back at the English with the warriors he could still muster. Now, though, with the ruins of Mystic still smoldering, the anger which had motivated the tribe for the past nine months was replaced with dismay. The display of English power and ruthlessness had shattered the will of the Pequot to sustain the fight any longer. Now the tribe had passed from fighting to surviving. The tribe began to dissolve with bands drifting away to seek sanctuary away from the English wrath. As a last impotent gesture they set fire to their own settlement and murdered those Mohegans belonging to Uncas' clan who lived among them.[190]

The fragments of the Pequot who did not seek shelter among other tribes were gradually pursued in follow on campaigns. Massachusetts and Connecticut soldiers continued to eliminate any remnants of the Pequot tribe they could find through June and July 1637. The Pequot hiding in the swamps and marshes throughout what had been their domain were gradually hunted down or turned themselves in. Neighboring tribes, the Mohegan, Niantic, and Narragansett absorbed some members of the Pequot.[191] Others, captured by the English, were most often sent into a life of slavery, as far away as the

---

[189] Underhill, 38.
[190] Radune, 34.
[191] Sylvester, 291-293.

West Indies.[192] The grand sachem Sassacus fled from Connecticut and sought shelter to the northwest in the land of the Mohawks. The Mohawks, no doubt hearing from traders of the conflict and the terrible English wrath, cast their lot with the English. They murdered Sassacus and many of the men he still had with him. Finally in October 1638 the victors in this savage little war signed a treaty in Hartford which attempted to formalize the final steps in the destruction of the Pequot nation and consolidation of the English position. [193]

The treaty between the English, the Narragansett and the Mohegan, also served English interests by seeming to establish conditions for peace between he two heirs to Pequot dominance, the Narragansett and the Mohegan. It further stipulated that that the small remaining remnant of the Pequot would be absorbed by the Mohegan, Niantic, and Narragansett tribes. Under the restrictions of the treaty those Pequot remaining in the region were forbidden from resettling abandoned villages, or even using the tribal name. The treaty also set aside these former Pequot lands as English. Finally this settlement attempted to solidify the English role as arbitrator for all significant disputes. The treaty bound the two tribes to "be guided by the judgment of the English, the latter would be justified in employing force to compel submission".[194] This last stipulation may have been a prudent gesture on the part of the English to preserve peace in the region and preempt disruptive competition between the Mohegan and the Narragansett.

By 1638 the subjugation of the Pequot tribe was essentially complete. The contact which had begun less than ten years earlier based on trade in shells and pelts had seen the

---

[192] Winthrop, 225-228.
[193] Cave, 160-161.
[194] Sylvester, 337.

tribe virtually erased from existence. The English moved to distribute the wealth in land and trade to their Indian allies and to the still small Connecticut colony. The land of the Pequots, largely ceded to the English in the treaty of Hartford, remained largely unsettled for much of the next decade. Events in England in the 1640s had cooled some of the migration to the New England colonies. Through the defeat of the Pequot the English had established themselves as the dominant "tribe" in New England. It would be another thirty-five years before any sizable challenge was made to English dominance in New England.

The Pequot people operated in a world of longstanding cultural norms which underwent profound upheaval in the years following their contact with the Europeans. The tribe experienced an increased thirst for power and position which was fed by the lucrative trade in furs and wampum along the rivers of Southern New England. Conflict between the tribes fueled the resentment which would later work against the Pequot. Increased contact also exposed their population to the ravages of foreign disease which significantly destabilized their own civic and cultural organization. Interaction with the Europeans exposed them to the experience and consequences of European state-competition, with its associated intrigues and violence. This essentially set the tribe on a course which they were ill prepared to navigate.

It cannot be overstated how inadequate the English intelligence was concerning the dispositions and intentions concerning many of the Indians. The English operated within the bias of their religious and cultural world view. They understood the Dutch and French motivations through their traditional dealings with them and the sharing of similar cultures. When faced with the varied tribes of New England they faced an enormous task of adaptation. The English had to establish and cultivate new relationships, overcome linguistic and cultural difficulties, and operate within a more challenging physical environment. There was no incentive for them to modify their biases since to do so would be a betrayal of the most deeply held religious beliefs.

Undoubtedly, some of the same challenges applied to the Pequot as well. It is important to remember that the principle parties in this sad affair had to make decisions based on prejudiced information from sources biased by diverse motives.

In 1636 decisions were made, by both sides, based on fear and biased assessments of the implications of those decisions. The English filtered their decisions through the lens offered by their interpretation of Christianity. The Pequot considered their dilemma through their own cultural biases. The rash and arrogant actions of a Puritan officer turned 'warlord' plunged the English frontier into a spasm of violence and retribution. Moderation yielded to fury and excess. Perhaps the Narragansett expressed their dismay best outside the Mystic fort, "mach it, mach it; that is, it is naught, it is naught, because it is too furious, and slaies [sic] too many men."[195] Those remarks, uttered about the violence of the English assault against the Mystic village, could have just as easily been uttered concerning the future of long-term English-Indian relations in New England.

---

[195] Underhill, "Captain John Underhill Justifies the attack on Mystic Village in the Pequot War (1637)," 43.

CHAPTER 4

A Chosen People

"We had sufficient light from the word of God for our proceedings." –John Underhill[196]

The English Puritans migrating to North America in the early to mid seventeenth century operated within an ideological model that gave priority to their particular religious worldview. Their positions on co-existence, compromise and conflict were influenced wholly or in part, by a theological view that as a people, they were set apart by God's own purposes.[197] This understanding of commission and all that flowed from it set the Puritans in opposition to the indigenous people of North America. This chapter will examine the Puritan mission in New England and how the New England tribes, specifically the Pequot, were treated in relation to the objective of Puritan expansion.

The Puritan movement in England sprung from the evolving mix of Protestant theology contending with the orthodoxy of the Roman Catholic Church in Europe. In England, the schism with the Catholic Church took on a decidedly political nature and the Church of England that evolved from that division remained closely tied to the political state. Puritans were, as discussed in chapter two, dissenters from that state-sanctioned Church of England. They differed by degrees in their closely held views.[198] In general

---

[196] John Underhill, "Captain John Underhill Justifies the Attack on Mystic Village in the Pequot War 1638," in *Major Problems in American Military History,* John W Chambers II and G.Kurt Piehler, eds. (Boston and New York: Houghton Mifflin Company, 1999), 41.
[197] Thomas J. Wertenbaker, *The First Americans 1607-1690,* (Chicago: Quadrangle Books, 1955), 91; John Cotton, "Gods Promise to His Plantation (1630)," Reiner Smolinski, ed. An Online Electronic Text Edition,http://digitalcommons.unl.edu/etas/22/ (accessed January 11, 2008), 7.
[198] Perry Miller, "The Puritan Way of Life," in *Puritanism in Early America,* George M. Waller, ed. (Boston: DC Heath and Company, 1950), 8-9.

however they developed a theological view that the official church was corrupt and did not operate in accordance with proper biblical teachings. It was the intent of the broader Puritan community to see this church ultimately reformed and reconciled with their beliefs. Even those who emigrated to the shores of New England in 1630 did not support a complete separation. For some English Protestants this was a vain hope and they chose a path of separation and complete rejection of the Church of England.[199]

Those Puritan Separatists who relocated to North America sprung from an intense strain of English Protestantism. They saw, in emigration, the opportunity to create a reformed civilization on the far shores of the Atlantic. The Separatists popularly referred to as Pilgrims in American history, surrendered hope of reconciliation with the English church. They all sought a degree of liberation from the state-church and a realization of their visions for the church and community.[200]

These English communities, both the Separatists of the Plymouth Colony and the Puritans of the Massachusetts Bay Colony, held beliefs that were decidedly Calvinist at the core, but which had evolved since John Calvin articulated his theological vision in Geneva in the early sixteenth century. Calvin, a French sixteenth century Protestant reformer and political thinker, heavily influenced Puritan theology. This cross-pollination in Protestant thought occurred prior to the reign of Elizabeth I (1558-1603) when some Protestant clergy, seeking sanctuary from the Catholic regime of Queen Mary and the attendant persecution, encountered his teachings in France and Switzerland.[201] At the

---

[199] Ezra Hoyt Byington, *The Puritan in England and New England* (Cambridge: University Press, 1896), 282.
[200] Miller, 5-7.
[201] Henry Albert Newman, *A Manual of Church History,* vol II, *Modern Church History (1517-1903)*,

core of Calvinist thinking was the belief that a strict reading of the Bible, both Old and New Testaments, should inform all aspects of the believer's life- religious, political, and social. Strict interpretation and reference to Biblical principles was not exclusively a Calvinist or Puritan practice. Nevertheless, in Puritan writing from the period, it is apparent that Scriptural instruction held a place of authority in matters religious and secular.

A detailed examination of Calvinist theology is not the aim of this paper, but some important distinctions in Calvinist thought found their way into Puritan theology. At its heart Calvin's theology upheld the idea that man is morally impotent and completely reliant on the absolute sovereignty of God for salvation. Calvin's theology was a severe theology that seemed to emphasize "the spirit of the Old Testament" and in practice and interpretation de-emphasize the more tolerant love of Christ for humankind emphasized the New Testament.[202]

One of the pillars in Calvinist doctrine was the concept of spiritual predestination. In this doctrine since God's knowledge and understanding were infallible, the salvation or damnation of individuals was already pre-ordained entering the world. This concept influenced the thinking of all devout church members. For the Puritan elect then, salvation was achieved and their time on earth was primarily oriented toward the realization of God's designs for humankind. The generation of Puritans who departed

---

(Philadelphia: American Baptist Publication Society, 1903), http://books. Google.com/books, (accessed February 10, 2008), 248.

[202] Phillip Schaff, *History of the Christian Church,* volume VIII, *Modern Christianity, The Swiss Reformation, 1882,* Christian Classics Ethereal Library 2002, http:// www. ccel. org/ccel/schaff/hcc8.html 9 (accessed February 8, 2008),178-179.

English shores to settle in New England believed that they were selected from among their nation "that they might be the seed for a new Christian nation". [203]

In general the Puritans held the conviction that natural man, un-Christianized, was separated from God and therefore in opposition to God. Since Puritanism rejected the doctrine of salvation through works, informed faith was central to the character of a true believer. Those who believed, through God's grace, could be saved. Put another way by William S. Simmons in his examination of Puritan and Indian culture, "The reborn self emerged only through a conversion experience that involved emotional as well as social levels of realization".[204] The Puritan then was expected, if conversion was genuine, to immerse himself in the doctrines of the church and organize his life around the same. This view held very serious implications for the native people of North America. Conversion therefore meant turning away from cultures developed over generations and implied the acceptance of ways that were essentially alien to the Indian experience. This expectation is not uniquely a Puritan or even Protestant view, but consideration of this fact provides some context for how the English approached the challenges of colonization.

The Puritans, even those sequestered in the New World, were not uniform in their beliefs. However, policy for the colonies was dominated by the leaders of the their movement, men like Governor John Winthrop, Reverend John Cotton, and John Endicott among others who adhered to the Puritan view of their place in the natural order, in

---

[203] Ibid., 324.
[204] William S. Simmons, "Cultural bias in the New England Puritans' Perception of Indians," *The William and Mary Quarterly,* 3rd ver., Vol. 38, no. 1 (January 1981), 56-72, www.jstor.org/ (accessed January 18, 2007), 58.

God's order.[205] These men of influence and learning were stout enough in their commitment to undertake the daunting task of emigration from their mother country to the edges of civilization. They were not men easily deterred or vacillating in their beliefs. As nineteenth century author, Ezra Hoyt Byington, writes of the Puritans, "Religious motives had the largest place in their lives."[206] They built on the bedrock of their beliefs a community more aligned with their deeply held convictions.

Albert Henry Newman states in his broad 1903 volume on the history of the Christian church, that Calvin also advocated the primacy of the church over the state, essentially urging that "The church must not only not be dependent on the state, it must rule the state"[207]. In the Puritan understanding and adaptation of Calvin's theology, a righteous society was one where the laws of the state supported and enforced the tenets of the church - in other words, a theocracy. In the fledgling colonies of New England, the church composed of the "Elect" assumed the pre-eminent position in framing the discussion of religious and political policy. Once they emigrated, the New England Puritans could apply their views as they grappled with the challenges of developing and executing colonial policies.[208]

For the Puritans the stark challenges of the New World also represented an environment of continual testing. They viewed this testing through a scriptural interpretation as an interaction with the living God. In that setting, they felt compelled by their beliefs to interpret and to act in a manner most closely fitting the overarching

---

[205] Thomas J. Wertenbaker, *The First Americans 1607-1690,* (Chicago: Quadrangle Books, 1955), 88-89.
[206] Byington, 282.
[207] Newman, 201.
[208] Byington, 282-283.

objective of Puritan settlement: the spreading of God's kingdom on earth. In John Winthrop's famous sermon, "A Model of Christian Charity," we can discern the complexity of thought harbored by the Puritan leader, but also the certainty and sense of purpose that he attached to their endeavor. Among his reasoning to his listeners to be resolute in their undertaking, he articulated several points, all tied to Biblical precedent.

> Thirdly, when God gives a special commission He looks to have it strictly observed in every article; When He gave Saul a commission to destroy Amaleck, He indented with him upon certain articles, and because he failed in one of the least, and that upon a fair pretense, it lost him the kingdom, which should have been his reward, if he had observed his commission.[209]

Then in the summation of his sermon, or thesis, he uttered his most famous remarks concerning their cause in the New World, Winthrop shared these doctrines, and ideals with many of those Englishmen who transplanted themselves from the home of their ancestors to a new and distant setting.

> The Lord will be our God, and delight to dwell among us, as His own people, and will command a blessing upon us in all our ways, so that we shall see much more of His wisdom, power, goodness and truth, than formerly we have been acquainted with. We shall find that the God of Israel is among us, when ten of us shall be able to resist a thousand of our enemies; when He shall make us a praise and glory that men shall say of succeeding plantations, "may the Lord make it like that of New England." For we must consider that we shall be as a city upon a hill. The eyes of all people are upon us. So that if we shall deal falsely with our God in this work we have undertaken, and so cause Him to withdraw His present help from us, we shall be made a story and a by-word through the world.[210]

---

[209] John Winthrop, "A Model of Christian Charity," John Beardsley, ed., http://religiousfreedom.lib.virginia.edu/sacred /charity.html, (accessed February 14, 2008).
[210] Ibid.

For many of these devout and committed men motivations of National pride, economic advancement, and exploratory zeal were subordinate to the central ethic of Protestant Christian expansion.

At the core of this enterprise was the establishment of new communities, or plantations in North America. Settlement of these lands would mean overcoming the natural and spiritual obstacles presented by the environment and indigenous people. The English settling in North America knew that the native people, however different, could not be ignored or wished away. They applied their understanding of the world to define and deal with the people they encountered.

Indians in Relation to the Puritan Objective

The English came to the New England in the seventeenth century with a cultural ideal as their vision. That ideal centered on the community of believers striving to broaden civilization's reach. Central to this civilization was the spread of the gospel, and the Puritan religious culture. The English settling along New England's shores did not view the Indian as an adversary on racial grounds. They considered the Indians as adversaries because they did not subordinate themselves to the civilization and culture offered by the English.

To the English, the Indians represented savage man, heathen and uncivilized. As such, their culture represented an obstacle to successful settlement. The Puritans wrestled with how to describe and overcome dynamic obstacle represented by the Indians and their culture. Central, so they thought, would be the requirement to civilize, and therefore convert, the Indians to the Puritan path. Puritan documents from the period testify to this view,

> It is the revealed will of God that the Gospel shall be preached in all nations, and though we know not whether those barbarians will receive it at first or not, yet it is a good work to serve God's providence in offering it to them (and this is the fittest to be done by God's own servants) for God shall have glory of it though they refuse it, and there is good hope that the posterity shall by this means be gathered into Christ's sheepfold. [211]

If the Indian refused conversion, and attendant absorption, then that rejection would only confirm the general European conviction that the Indians were pre-ordained for damnation and subjugation by the civilized and godly champions of Christendom.

The Puritans acknowledged that the Indians were the natural inhabitants of the land. Nevertheless, they also believed that Protestant Europeans were ordained to inherit this land. In a preserved sermon, *God's Promise to His Plantation*, the Reverend John Cotton described three means by which God "makes room for a people". God blesses rightful military conquest, softens the hearts of those already inhabiting the land, or provides a land with sufficient vacancy to support the migrants.[212] Consistently they turned to their interpretation of scriptural guidance and precedent to justify their "divine

---

[211] John Winthrop, "Reasons for the Plantation in New England ca.1628," Marcia Elaine Stewart, ed., http://www.winthropsociety.org/doc_reasons.php (accessed February 14, 2008).
  The editor notes that the document was found among the papers of Governor John Winthrop. Other abridged versions are in existence but may be ascribed to Rev. John White, John Winthrop or Rev. Francis Higginson. "The Rev. John White probably conceived the initial nine arguments, but we suspect, due to the legal style of its arguments, that Winthrop has here substantially amplified it to its present form with the addition of the objections and answers. In any event, it is surely an expression of Winthrop's own views on the subject, and is of great significance in revealing the motivation of the colonists." Marcia Elaine Stewart.
[212] John Cotton, "Gods Promise to His Plantation (1630)," Reiner Smolinski, ed., An Online Electronic Text Edition, http://digitalcommons.unl.edu/etas/22/ (accessed January 11, 2008), 4.

right"[213] to the land, and by logical extension, the inhabitants. Puritan writings prior to their departure from England addressed a series of objections regarding the endeavor.

> *Objection I — We have no warrant to enter upon that land, which has been so long possessed by others.*
> *Answer 1:*
> That which lies common, and has never been replenished or subdued, is free to any that possess and improve it; for God hath given to the sons of men a double right to the earth — there is a natural right and a civil right. The first right was natural when men held the earth in common, every man sowing and feeding where he pleased....[214]

The author, most likely John Winthrop, concludes this line of reasoning with the following:

> ...As for the natives in New England, they enclose no land, neither have they any settled habitation, nor any tame cattle to improve the land by, and so have no other but a natural right to those countries. So if we leave them sufficient for their own use, we may lawfully take the rest, there being more than enough for them and for us.[215]

John Winthrop's cultivated this view prior to his own interaction with the Indians. These assumptions were based on widely circulated accounts from the Virginia and Plymouth colonies, in addition to the traders who frequented the shores. A shortcoming in the Puritans considerations prior to colonization was their failure to foresee the disruptive impact their migration would have for native societies.[216] In fairness however, their intellectual framework simply did not allow for that consideration.

The English generally recognized that they must approach their dealings with the Indians with some trappings of honor and justice. Bitter experiences in Virginia, where

---

[213] Roy Harvey Pearce, "The "Ruines of Mankind": The Indian and the Puritan Mind,*" Journal of the History of Ideas*, 13, no. 2 (April 1952), 200-217, www.jstor.org/ (accessed November 12, 2007), 203.
[214] Winthrop, "Reasons for the Plantation in New England ca.1628,"
[215] Ibid.
[216] Karen Ordahl Kupperman, "English Perceptions of Treachery, 1583-1640: The Case of the American 'Savages'," *The Historical Journal*, 20, no. 2 (June 1977), 263-287. www.jstor.org/ (accessed November 10, 2007), 274-275.

haughty and rough treatment by the English had alienated some of the Indians, motivated cautionary statements from investors and church leaders. While they would not go so far as to recognize the sovereignty of the Indians in the European sense, they did recognize that poor treatment would imperil their greater mission in New England.[217]

Indigenous cultures, uncivilized, presented the chief obstacle to conversion and salvation. The Puritans saw in the Indian's culture man clearly separated from God. There was no theological middle ground acknowledged. The Indians then, as natural-man, existed separated from the grace of God and therefore in the sway of the opponent- the Devil. Some men like Roger Williams and Thomas Morton, became sympathetic advocates for the Indians, describing the Indians' culture in terms that often reflected favorably.[218] Yet despite their complementary accounts, the Indian culture, in the Puritan view, remained an adversarial culture. Only the Indians' submission and adaptation could bridge this gulf.

In the opening decades of English settlement, religious conversion of Indians was

---

[217] Ibid.
[218] William S. Simmons, "Cultural bias in the New England Puritans' Perception of Indians," *The William and Mary Quarterly,* 3rd Ser., vol. 38, no. 1 (January1981), 56-72. www.jstor.org/ (accessed January 18, 2007), 65-67.; Roger Williams, "A Key into the Language of America: Or a Help to the Language of the Natives, in that part of America, called New England. Together with brief Observations of the Customs, Manners, and Worships, &c. of the aforesaid Natives, in Peace and War, in Life and Death," Collections of the Massachusetts Historical Society, vol.III (Boston: Apollo Press), http://capecodhistory.us/19th/MHS1794.htm#2039 (accessed January 4, 2008).
Both Englishmen fell outside of the Puritan orthodoxy; both were exiles from their English communities. Morton a Church of England man was not favorably regarded in the Plymouth colony. He maintained cordial relations with local Indians at the expense of his relationship with the Plymouth men. Roger Williams settled among the Narragansett people following his exile from the Bay colony for differences of theology. However positive their impressions of native cultures were they could not make the final leap and disregard the idea that the devil and witchcraft retained influence and importance in Indian culture and religion.

not a widespread occurrence. It is likely that many Indian nations, like the Pequot, operated under the idea that they could deal with the Dutch and English as they had with other regional tribes. There is little evidence that points to an internal debate among any of the Indians concerning the cultural impact of settlement and expansion. We do have evidence that when the English encountered resistance that opposition confirmed the "satanic" influence among the natives in Puritan eyes.[219] Even Indian cooperation in trade, politics, and warfare did not soften the root English view. William Simmons notes in his examination of English cultural biases that Indian assistance or even generosity were evidence of God's grace to the English rather than any redeeming quality among the Indians themselves.[220]

Tensions mounted across southern New England between and among the tribes and with the English as settlement expanded. These tensions accelerated into acts of violence, and then outright warfare. In the Puritan interpretation of events, this conflict became a complex pivotal act in the contest between the forces of Christ and the forces allied with the devil. By 1636, the Pequot most potently and immediately represented the forces of evil. By extinguishing this threat, they were executing God's plan for the wilderness.[221]

War comes to the Wilderness Zion

"Thus did the Lord Judge among the Heathen, filling the Place with dead Bodies!"-

---

[219] Pearce, 204; Simmons, 67.
[220] Simmons, 66. See also Edward Johnson, *Wonder-Working Providence of Sions Savior in New England*, J. Franklin Jameson, ed. (New York, Charles Schribner and Sons, 1910), http://books.Google.com/books, (accessed January 21, 2008),79-80.
[221] Pearce, 201-202.

Captain John Mason[222]

The Puritan's theological framework allowed that, "...no Nation is to drive out another without speciall [sic] Commission from heaven, such as the *Israelites* had..." this interpretation retained a caveat, "unless [sic] the Natives do unjustly wrong them, and will not recompence [sic] the wrongs done in peaceable sort, & then they may right themselves by lawfull [sic] war, and subdue the Countrey [sic] unto themselves."[223]. With the John Stone and John Oldham murders, the Pequot had set themselves in opposition to the English. Practical, matters of trade and conversion became subordinate. They perceived the immediate threat to their community to be present in the savage Pequot.

In 1636, the English fulfilled, in their minds, the obligation to offer the Pequot an opportunity to atone for the murders. The Pequot prevarication in this matter set them apart for destruction. With clerical blessing, the English then embarked on their punitive expeditions. By the time John Mason led his force against the Pequot at Mystic there was no turning back. In the Puritan mind, there could be no peace with the enemies of God.

The English went to war in 1636 against the Pequot not merely to subdue a recalcitrant people. They took on the mantel of a new "chosen" people, agents acting within the will of God. The logical extension of this thought was that the unconverted Pequot who resisted them were the infidel occupiers of a holy land, intended by God's will, for the chosen people. It was a small step for the English to turn to the force of arms,

---

[222] John Mason, *A Brief History of the Pequot War: Especially of the Memorable Taking of their Fort at Mistick in Connecticut in 1637* (Boston: Keeland and T. Green, 1736), http://books.Google.com/books, (accessed February 10, 2008),30.
[223] Cotton, 6.

as the Israelites had in Canaan.[224] The Pequot seemed to represent a threat and obstacle to their mission in New England. They became enemies of the English, and therefore, assumed enemies of God. It was in this setting that military men, John Underhill, John Mason, Lion Gardiner, among others became capable holy warriors for the Puritan cause

---

[224] Joshua. 6:21,24 [King James Version]

CHAPTER 5

CULTURES OF WAR

Even before Captain John Mason and his force of English militia and Indian allies destroyed the Pequot village at Mystic the status of the Pequot as an independent Indian society was decided. Indispensible to understanding the downfall of the Pequot is a consideration of what author Adam J. Hirsch calls the "interaction of military cultures."[225] This examination of their disparate military cultures and technology enters into any serious discussion of the war. As he points out in his essay *The Collision of Military Cultures in Seventeenth-Century New England,* the greater "history of conflict" between the Indians and the English should involve a comparison of the two adversaries' military traditions. This will set the conditions for a more detailed consideration of the two key factors that facilitated English military superiority in southern New England. The first and frequently cited factor addresses the possession of advanced technology by the English. This provided them with tools for both protection and killing relative to their opponents. Second, and more importantly, the English possessed a cadre of experienced soldiers who were well versed in a centuries old culture of warfare. Many of the Englishmen who fought this war were well versed in a sophisticated military tradition developed and passed down through generations. This tradition determined the harsh English response to conflict and provided the English colonists with a decisive advantage against the Pequot.

---

[225] Adam J. Hirsch, "The Collision of Military Cultures in Seventeenth-Century New England," *The Journal of American History* 74, no. 4 (March 1988), 1187.

When war came between the Pequot and English in 1636, the English colonies in Massachusetts, Plymouth and Connecticut were full of military "novices".[226] They relied on the skills and courage of a drilled militia led by veteran officers to carry the fight to the enemy. When the Puritan colonists committed themselves to war against the Pequot, they largely followed military customs and practices developed on the varied battlefields of Europe. In a similar fashion, the Indians they fought against also had a military tradition developed and ingrained in their larger culture. In this collision of cultures, there was no middle ground, no mutually accepted code governing the conduct of war.[227] The experience of the Pequot War illustrates that warfare between the Indians and the English was a savage affair.

The English were not an exceptionally bloodthirsty people by the standards of their day, but they had learned about killing on a scale never before witnessed in North America. They drew from a rich culture of martial tradition and practice. Centuries of warfare on their own island, mainland Europe, and Ireland had exposed them to conflicts that could generate "extraordinary levels of violence".[228] A pool of experienced professional military men existed all across the continent in the early seventeenth century. The period of the late sixteenth and early seventeenth centuries were marked by increasing intensity and scale of warfare in Europe. Larger portions of the population either found themselves under arms or actively sought to make a living serving as

---

[226] Guy Chet, *Conquering the American Wilderness-The Triumph of European Warfare in the Colonial Northeast* (Amherst, MA: University of Massachusetts Press, 2003), 11.

[227] Ronald D. Karr, "Why Should You Be So Furious?: The Violence of the Pequot War," *The Journal of American History* 85, no. 3 (December 1998), 879,909.

[228] Ibid.,907.

soldiers.[229]

By the standards of the day a professional may have served under contract more than a single sovereign or state. As warfare grew in sophistication and scope the states of Europe often turned to these contract soldiers to supplement their own formation or fill the need for a specialized skill set such as engineering or artillery. In general these were men skilled in the art and science of combat and acquainted with the military practices of preceding generations.[230] This pool of men was to provide the early colonists with military leadership during a crucial period in their development.

The first colonists to establish their settlements on the New England coast were aware of the hazards they faced in their endeavors. These colonists could not rely on trained regiments dispatched from the mother country to secure the frontier of English and Christian expansion. They would be responsible for their own defense. Instead, to aid them in this task they turned to members of their community with experience and skill at arms. If they could find no such men from within their church, they hired professional soldiers to train and lead their militias.[231]

Colonial leaders commissioned men like Myles Standish, John Underhill, John Mason, Lion Gardiner, and Daniel Patrick to train and lead their novice militias. These men were generally accepted by the community despite often not being members of the

---

[229] Geoffrey Parker, "Dynastic War," in *The Cambridge History of Warfare*, Geoffrey Parker, ed. (New York: Cambridge University Press, 2005), 148-149.

[230] Parker,150,157; Jenks, Tudor. *Captain Myles Standish,* (New York, Century Company, 1905) 38. In Europe, the transmission of information through the written word enhanced the understanding of military culture. A well read European would have access to numerous sources of military theory. Literate Europeans, like Miles Standish, could look to their family history, Biblical accounts, and in some cases the classics for background on their profession. This expanded their familiarity with the art and science of warfare beyond their own personal experience.

[231] Chet, 13.

church. What these men had in common were military skills forged during their experience as officers in the English military component supporting the Protestant cause in the Netherlands.[232] European warfare was evolving during a period of prolonged struggle between the mid-sixteenth century until early in the seventeenth century. One of the most ruthless theaters of combat during the period was in the Netherlands where the Dutch and their Protestant allies fought against the Roman Catholic Empire of Spain in a struggle for Dutch independence.[233] In that setting a generation of English mercenary soldiers developed their skills and their understanding of war on mainland Europe.

The war fought in Northwest Europe was a bloody affair pitting the interests of dynastic powerhouses like Spain against the emerging interests and nationalism of the Dutch confederation. During this same period, there was a shift in the ideology behind warfare. Increasingly the justification for warfare and unrest on the continent assumed decidedly religious overtones. The Protestant reformation and its challenge to the established religious and political order was a powerful destabilizing influence in Europe. War on the continent frequently pitted armies against each other motivated not simply by money or politics but increasingly infused with a sense of divine purpose, and license, for their cause.[234] Rulers of the period began to equate "…their own interests, and those of the lands they ruled with God…"[235] Monarchs, clergy, and commanders encouraged the views that intensified factional religious exclusivity. The culture of war in Europe was transforming, from dynastic wars for power and possessions to conflicts understood more

---
[232] Ibid., 14.
[233] Karr, 891; Parker, 155.
[234] Parker, 162-164.
[235] Ibid.,164.

frequently in ideological terms as well.

The European way of war was much more than the use of firearms and horse cavalry. Increasingly the justification and appeal to wage war had its' own attendant ideology that encouraged the fury of combat rather than restrain it. Soldiers fought not simply for monarchs and honor but deeply held religious beliefs. The wars of this period often involved interpretations of the Christian faith as much as they involved dynastic or national power. The Protestant English soldiers who honed their skills in this ideological environment brought these influences with them to the New World.

Once ashore in the new colonies these military men set about to instill the raw militias with the discipline they had mastered in the Netherlands fighting for the Dutch. The English colonies in North America could not support their own standing armies. Instead they developed prepared militias, trained to answer the call to arms in the defense of their communities. Massachusetts Bay Colony went so far as to establish legislation governing the conduct of these early militia formations.[236] The hired professional soldiers the Puritan English brought to New England trained their fellow colonists on the basic skills, and discipline common to most European soldiers of the period.[237]

The farmers, artisans, and laborers filling the colonies military establishment were acquainted with the tactics appropriate to their situation and the tools at hand. They were trained to handle edged weapons, and pikes, singly and in formation. Collective drill

---

[236] Chet, 21. During the first decade of the Puritan Massachusetts Bay colony legislation was passed which mandated town watches, militia drills, and material preparedness for all subordinate communities. The intent was to establish a system of defense that would facilitate mutual support of communities in the event of a threat or attack from Native Americans or European rivals.

[237] Parker, 158. Massachusetts Bay's militia companies were all led by veterans of the Dutch Army and trained in the methods and tactics refined by the Dutchman, Maurice of Nassau whose innovations in small unit tactics sought to maximize the effectiveness of firearms against opposing formations.

often involved the basics training with the cumbersome firearms of the period. Just as with the edged weapons, members of the militia were taught to form ranks, and respond to firing commands familiar to a soldier in a standing army. The intent behind this was to maximize the ability of the organization to form, discharge their weapons, reload, and reposition in an effective manner. These small militias were trained in the tasks deemed essential to defend small settlements, and fixed positions.

Due in large part to the nature of the terrain, their tools, and their numbers the militia were best suited to the tactical defensive rather than any large-scale coordinated actions. Some scholars, considering evidence from later conflicts like the King Phillips War of 1676, have argued that the early colonists had tactics that were unsuitable to combat in North America and that they subsequently departed from their European roots. It was consistent with European practice to seek a positional advantage from which their formations could deliver high volumes of fire against their opponent. In the New World, this imperative grew in importance because of the size and resources of the forces involved.[238] Closer examination of the experiences of the first New England settlements and the conflict with the Pequot does not support the idea that the colonial militia were struggling to develop appropriate doctrine for their situation although experience shows they were able to adapt their tactics when required.

From the beginning, the first colonists maintained a fear that a sudden raid by Indian war parties could sweep them away. This concern was upheld by their first skirmish, which occurred in December 1620 against a small party of Nauset warriors. Standish led a nine-man reconnaissance party scouting the western shore of Cape Cod,

---
[238] Chet, 30-32.

near present day Eastham. The party landed and established a small camp on the shore along a tidal creek. Standish urged the erection of a protective barricade to secure their small site and maintained an armed sentry through the night. On the morning of December 8, the Nauset attacked from the nearby woods. The English stood their ground and drove the attackers off. Guy Chet dissects the encounter and argues that it demonstrates, on a limited tactical level, European tactics adapted to realities of their new frontier. Standish had established defensive posture and "In keeping with European defensive tactics" which sought to force the opponent into conducting a costly assault of a fortified position, Standish ordered, "…the defenders at the barricade were commanded to maintain a steady rotation of fire".[239] It is unclear if there were any Indian casualties from this encounter. The English were able to leverage their technological advantage into fear-power that dissuaded the Indians from pressing the attack. This encounter was a qualified success. It at least demonstrated to the Nauset that the Englishmen would stand their ground and fight.

The New England Indians had their own caste of warriors and their own associated traditions of combat. Indian warfare in New England did not share the same broad and intense motivations as the Europeans. The Indians also lacked the powerful religious motivations that had influenced warfare in the "Old World". As author Adam Hirsch notes, "Given ample land and a system of values by and large indifferent to material accumulation, the New England tribes rarely harbored the economic and

---

[239] Nathaniel Philbrick, *Mayflower, A Story of Courage Community and War* (London: Viking Penguin Group, 2006),70-73; Bradford, 69-70; Chet 16-17.

political ambitions that fueled European warfare."[240] This shaped the military culture of the various tribes. Hirsch is partially correct in his assertion regarding Indian ambitions, but during the first decades of European colonization this aspect of culture had begun to change. The Indians intensified their political and economic competition in southern New England. However, at the time of the Pequot War the traditional modes of combat still predominated.

Observers from the period present some excellent illustrations of the native military tradition and practice that existed in southern New England. Warfare was more often a matter of retaliation for "isolated acts of violence" than a struggle for domination or conquest. The aims of warfare were usually quite limited as exemplified in the Pequot involvement in the killing of John Stone. They framed this as a retaliatory act for Dutch violence against their tribe. In this setting of relative restraint, violence might abate once the desire for revenge or punishment was satisfied.[241]

This is not to assert that warfare for the Indians was a casual affair. Individual combat for the Native Americans could be as ruthless as the combat of Europeans. Individual standards and definitions of honor and bravery differed little from individual European standards.[242] Moreover, they were just as ingrained in the larger culture of the society. Organizations for war reflected the imperatives of the tribe or clan and the dynamics of persuasive leadership. When the collision came with the English, the Indians

---

[240] Hirsch, 1190.
[241] Ibid.
[242] Thomas Morton, *"Manners and Customs of the Indians (of New England) 1637,"* Oliver J. Thatcher, ed., *The Library of Original Sources*, vol. V, *9th to 16th Centuries* (Milwaukee: University Research Extension Co., 1907), http://www.fordham.edu/halsall/mod/1637morton.html (accessed August 28 2007).

naturally organized and conducted themselves in the customs derived from their own historical experience of war.

In the tribal societies of southern New England, the practice of warfare did not demand a specific division of labor as had evolved elsewhere in the world. Many populations were relatively small and the economic demands of the community generally precluded a specific caste devoted to warfare. This reality influenced the duration, conduct, and intensity of Native American warfare. The male population fully participated in the subsistence of the tribe.[243] Yet when required, or more accurately, persuaded, the able-bodied male participated in the tribe's military activities. Communities simply could not support lengthy campaigns or standing armies. Warfare was still widely regarded as a grave matter for the tribe or clan.

Despite its more limited nature, armed conflict between tribes could imperil the political independence and economic well-being of the group. There is no evidence to suggest that the Indians engaged in the wide-scale slaughter that often accompanied the European clash of armies.[244] According to observers from the period Indians tended to be selective about when to engage adversaries in combat.[245] Puritan Edward Johnson, founder of Woburn and witness to negotiations with the Narragansett, remarked on the solemnity of deliberations on the matter of war: "It was a matter of much wonderment to the English to see how solidly and wisely these savage people did consider of the weighty

---

[243] William Cronon, *Changes in the Land: Indians, Colonists, and the Ecology of New England* (New York: Hill and Wang, 1983), 41-42.
[244] Karr, 876, 878, 882-883.
[245] Morton, " These savages are not apt to quarrel one with another; yet such has been the occasion that a difference has happened which has grown to that height that it has not been reconciled otherwise than by combat,…"

undertaking of a War".[246] Roger Williams observed a similar prudent hesitancy in his study of the Narragansett tribe;

> The mocking between their great ones is a great kindling of wars amongst them: Yet I have known some of their chiefs say, "What should I hazard the lives of my precious subjects, them and theirs, to kindle a fire which no man knows how far and how long it will burn, for the barking of a dog?"[247]

This deliberation on the matter does attest to the fact that although warfare in Indian culture lacked the intensity of the European battlefield they understood the effects of the universal human experience of violence and did not take the matter lightly.

Of course, warfare was not always avoidable and when it did come, the various tribes in southern New England generally employed similar tactics. In some cases individual combat settled matters. In those instances the process witnessed by Thomas Morton was probably typical;

> …the two champions prepared for the fight, with their bows in hand and a quiver full of arrows at their backs, they have entered into the field; the challenger and challenged have chosen two trees, standing within a little distance of each other; they have cast lots for the choice of the trees, then either champion setting himself behind his tree watches an advantage to let fly his shafts, and to gall his enemy; there they continue shooting at each other; if by chance they espie [sic] any part open, they endeavor to gall the combatant in that part, and use much agility in the performance of the task they have in hand. Resolute they are in the execution of their vengeance, when once they have begun; and will in no wise be daunted, or seem to shrink though they do catch a clap with an arrow, but fight it out in this manner until one or both be slain.[248]

---

[246] Edward Johnson, *Wonder-Working Providence of Sions Savior in New England*, J. Franklin Jameson, ed. (New York, Charles Schribner and Sons, 1910), 163.

[247] Roger Williams, "A Key into the Language of America: Or an Help to the Language of the Natives, in that part of America, called New England. Together with brief Observations of the Customs, Manners, and Worships, &c. of the aforesaid Natives, in Peace and War, in Life and Death," Collections of the Massachusetts Historical Society, vol.III, (Boston: Apollo Press), http://capecodhistory.us/19th/MHS1794.htm#2039 (accessed January 4, 2008), 235.

[248] Morton

The Indians generally observed a cultural prohibition against killing their adversary's women and children.[249] War parties often took women and children captive and even adopted them into the tribe as a means to recoup losses or expand increase the size and power of the tribe. Treatment of male captives was another matter altogether. It was routine for Indians to engage in ritualistic torture of male captives. Sometimes these captives survived these ordeals but quite often they did not. Hirsch argues that these acts of ritualized cruelty may have served as an "emotional compensation for the prescribed restraint in combat." These acts of torture often horrified Europeans, even those accustomed to tremendous violence on the battlefield. Torture remained accepted as a technique of European jurisprudence, however "martial tradition held it dishonorable".[250] The torture of captured Englishmen during the Pequot War enhanced the perception that the Indian was a fiendish opponent who operated outside of what the Europeans considered honorable conduct.

In combat, it was natural for the Indians to employ similar tactics to those they employed while hunting game. Their technology for killing and protection was unsophisticated and did not require procedural adaptations to be effective. War parties took advantage of their well-developed skills for moving on the land and operating in small bands while stalking their opponents. Indian warfare was inherently offensive in orientation. As Chet explains, the Indians were generally "unencumbered by sedentary

---

[249] Lion Gardener, "Relation of the Pequot Warres," W.N. Chattin Carlton, ed. (Hartford: Hartford Press, 1901), http://digitalcommons.unl.edu/etas/38, (accessed October 24, 2007), 15. The Pequot approached the Saybrook fort at one point and attempted to gauge the English attitude about continued hostilities and any limitations on fighting particularly regarding women and children.
[250] Hirsch,1192; Winthrop, 194.

communities" and therefore not compelled to maintain their position on the battlefield."[251] Therefore, raids and ambushes were the norm as opposed to mass combat, or siege craft.

By the time of the Pequot War, the English were familiar with many of the Indian practices. For the English fighting in the New World during the first two decades of settlement, this meant some adaptation in small unit tactics had to occur, but this did not invalidate their basic tactical approaches to small unit action. Captain John Underhill explains that during the Block Island raid the English had modified some of their tactics to enhance their own effectiveness.

> I would not have the world wonder at the great number of Commanders to so few men, but know that the Indians fight farre [sic] differs from the Christian practice [sic], for they most commonly divide themselves into small bodies, so that we are forced to neglect our usuall [sic] way and to subdivide our divisions to answer theirs..[252]

The professionals trained the inexperienced militia in the procedures of drill that were useful to maximize the effectiveness of firearms and steel weapons. The Indians for their part gradually gained an appreciation for the effectiveness of European weapons and protection that these relatively small bands of Englishmen could bring to the field. Adaptation to the technological challenges the Europeans presented was beyond the ability of the tribes to achieve independently.

---

[251] Chet, 30; Hirsch 1191.
[252] John Underhill, *"Newes from America; Or, A New and Experimentall Discoverie of New England; Containing, A Trve Relation of Their War-like Proceedings These Two Yeares Last Past, with a Figure of the Indian Fort, or Palizado,"* Paul Royster, ed., www.digitalcommons.unl.edu/etas/37/ (accessed October 24, 2007), 3.

Musketballs and Arrowheads

It is useful to consider the contrast in military technology that unavoidably shaped the fighting between the Pequot and the English. In the first decades of English colonization, the Native Americans possessed adequate tools to engage their traditional enemies in deadly combat.[253] Wooden war clubs, stone, bone, and iron knives, and widespread use of the bow and arrow were the primary weapons in the Indian's arsenal. By this time, the Indians had begun to acquire European firearms, powder, and some iron weapons, but their use was not widespread enough to present a credible threat to European dominance in war making technology. The Indians gradually began to develop some skill with the use of firearms but they lacked the technical skill to repair them when damaged. They also relied on trade with the Europeans for gunpowder.[254] Significantly there was little indigenous development in the field of protection. The tribes of southern New England lacked the iron and heavy leather armor of the Europeans, possessing nothing sufficient to withstand a cutlass blow or a lead ball. The nature of their warfare and culture had not encouraged the evolution of systems of protection like European armor or the quilted armor of the Indian empires of Central and South America.[255]

By the time of the Pequot War, the Indians understood the power of European firearms. They were also aware that the heavily armored Europeans made poor targets for their arrows and were difficult to kill. In fact, the English colonists of this period clad

---

[253] Jacob Abbot, *Abbot's American Histories,* vol. I, *Aboriginal America,* (New York: Sheldon and Company, 1860), 184-185.; Philbrick, 72.

[254] James B. Whisker, *Arms Makers of Colonial America* (London and Toronto; Associated University Press, 1992) http://books.google.com/books (accessed April 11, 2008), 19.

[255] Jared Diamond, *Guns, Germs, And Steel, The Fates of Human Societies* (New York: W.W. Norton and Company, 1999), 75-76.

themselves in iron armored vests or coats of heavy leather for protection even as these articles faded from use in Europe.[256] These efforts were not foolproof but did reduce the casualties suffered by the English. John Underhill was spared injury by his helmet during his first combat encounter with the Block Island Indians, "my selfe [sic] received an arrow through my coate [sic] sleeve, a second against my Helmet on the forehead..."[257] If instead of arrows, the Indians had been able to fire a volley of lead shot the iron helmet may not have saved him.

Interestingly in this war, the English did not hesitate to employ a devastating and rather indiscriminate weapon against the Indians – fire. During the raid on Block Island, they burnt villages, fields, and possessions. Then in Mystic, Mason employed fire to destroy the Indian village and its inhabitants. The Pequot had access to this same tool but only used it on one occasion to destroy some structures near Fort Saybrook.[258] The most reliable explanation for this restraint in the use of fire as a weapon, particularly used against entire villages, was that it was not yet widely viewed as a useful tool in the Indian's way of war.

European weaponry had proliferated somewhat among various tribes along with increased European trade, enough to worry the English. Some of the English were concerned that as the Indians gained skill with firearms and developed the capability to maintain and supply them they would imperil the European position.[259] William Bradford

---

[256] Hirsch, 1196.
[257] Underhill, 4.
[258] Cave, 112,129,150.
[259] See Whisker, "In the eastern portion of what is today the United States firearms had a greater impact on Native Americans than any other product introduced by the European intruders.", 19. As trade relationships with Europeans expanded the Indians recognized the utility of firearms and they began to replace traditional weapons in use for hunting and warfare. The French were probably the first to introduce

of the Plymouth colony expressed considerable anxiety in this regard. He criticized those who not only supported the growing market for guns but also provided the means to make powder and shot, "And these things have been done in the same times when some of their neighbours [sic] and friends are daily killed by Indians or are in danger thereof and live but at the Indians mercy."[260] Bradford voiced his concern at a time of relative peace before the outbreak of war with the Pequot. As Adam Hirsch discusses in his essay, "The differences between musket balls and arrowheads were plain to see, but the disparities between colonial and Indian military strategy would not come to light until they were directly experienced."[261]

A Savage Affair: The English Way of War

The Pequot were on the receiving end of a strategy that placed a premium on ability of the English military force to terrorize and destroy their opponents. As Ronald Karr identifies in his essay on the Pequot War the instructions given to John Endecott by the political and religious leadership of Massachusetts Bay had clearly indicated he was to "proceed against entire Indian tribes, not just their armies."[262] This was not the warfare of recognized armies in Europe. This was the punitive warfare waged against "rebels,

---

weapons in large quantities to Northern Tribes, the Dutch followed suit, and then the English. Trade in weaponry upset balances of power, increased the destructiveness of combat, and replaced traditional skills within a generation as making bows and arrows became irrelevant. The author also points out that the Indians never really mastered the skills required to produce usable quantities of powder or make comprehensive repairs to firearms.

[260] Bradford, 206-207.
[261] Hirsch, 1196.
[262] Karr, 902; Cave 109.

heretics, or infidels."[263]

Hirsch argues that the failure of the Indians to meet the English in direct battle motivated the English to employ other, harsher, tactics to defeat their opponents.[264] This view may be lacking a complete consideration of European approaches to combat against those considered outside of the full protection of the recognized laws of warfare. In Europe by 1630 the ethics of warfare or "codes of combat" had evolved to recognize distinctions in the conduct of war against a sovereign's armies and noncombatants. Dutch author Hugo Grotius developed a code, published in 1625, to direct the conduct of warfare in Christian states. His work, *De Jure Belli ac Pacis Libri Tres* (On the Laws of War and Peace). The excesses that occurred during the long war between the Dutch and Spanish heavily influenced his work. In practice, of course the rules were frequently ignored. As broad as his coverage was the rules did not seem to apply to all circumstances. In the New World the Europeans most often cited the Biblical Old Testament as their guide and drew on their experiences fighting heathens and infidels in the Mediterranean basin.[265] The body of ethical thought influencing combat also recognized the distinction between fighting a formal, or conventional opponent, and fighting an unconventional enemy. There was a precedent in the English tradition of war for this sort of campaigning outside of their military adventures in the Netherlands.

---

[263] Ibid.,902; Hirsch, 1208. The author quotes from Reverend Solomon Stoddard, "If the Indians were as other people are, and did manage their war fairly after the manner of other nations, it might be looked upon as inhumane to pursue them."

[264] Hirsch, 1209.

[265] This evolving law of war is described in great length in a translation of Hugo Grotius, On *the Law of War and Peace, 1625,* trans. A. C. Campbell (London, 1814), http://www.constitution.org/gro/djbp.htm (accessed January 4, 2008) Chapter II, *Inquiry into the lawfulness of war*; Diamond,69.

Ronald Dale Karr argues convincingly that the nature and conduct of warfare in Ireland during the sixteenth and early seventeenth centuries can be useful in understanding their later approach to war against the North American Indians. During the reign of Elizabeth I, the English fought against determined resistance to assert their control over the island. English armies faced opponents who did not fight in the accepted European fashion. As Kerr summarizes, "Ambushes, raids, and guerilla attacks on rough terrain characterized traditional Irish warfare."[266] Significantly, the English regarded their opponents' not so much as skilled fighters but as rebels to the legitimate authority of England.[267] This view would frame the English response.

During the conflict in question, known as the Desmond rebellions, both sides cast aside restraint in their zeal to terrorize and defeat their opponent. Rebel Irish forces, with the aid of enlisted Spanish and Italian Catholic soldiers, pledged to make war against the forces of the "Heretic Queen".[268] The opposing sides were ideological foes who each viewed the other with profound contempt. Both sides fought in a manner beyond the accepted norms of battlefield practice between states or regular armies. In this setting, it was acceptable to take hostages, lay waste to towns, and kill declared enemies regardless

---

[266] Kerr, 886.
[267] Edmund Spenser, *A Veue of the present state of Irelande,* [1596] prepared from the text found in Grosart[1894] (The University of Oregon, 1997), http://www.uoregon.edu /~rbear/veue1.html (accessed January 12, 2008). Spenser wrote a work of prose titled, *A View of the Present State of Ireland*. It was not published until the middle of the seventeenth century for reasons that are not clear. In his work he argued to pacify Ireland the English must destroy the native language, and divisive customs. Naturally, the broad application of state sanctioned violence against combatants and non-combatants alike sought to accomplish this absolute subjugation of the native people He had served in Ireland during campaigns in the sixteenth century and was involved with the brutal suppression of the Desmond Rebellions. The Desmond rebellions occurred in Southern Ireland and pitted the English against local nobility resistant to English rule. Additionally there was the element of religious struggle as well with the Irish being Roman Catholic and the Elizabethan English being Protestant. The English did not differentiate between soldier and civilian during the campaign. http://en.wikipedia.org/wiki/Edmund_Spenser [accessed January12, 2008.]
[268] Mary Teresa Hayden, *A Short History of the Irish People from the Earliest Times to 1920* (London: Longmans, Green and Co. 1922), 235-240.

of age, gender or status.[269] This heritage was a significant part of the conception of war that the English would bring with them to the New World and unleash against the Indians.

The most compelling influence for the English ferocity against Indians in New England came directly from a closer source, the Virginia colony. One of the architects of English-Indian relations in Virginia was Ralph Lane. Lane was a military man primarily with experience in Ireland. His policies of forceful coercion included martial displays and hostage taking among the Indians. Karen Ordahl Kupperman argues that Lane's view of the Indians as savages, dangerous and untrustworthy, motivated the initial English behavior and therefore set conditions for increased intercultural hostility.[270]

The view of the Indians as a clever and vicious threat became a self-fulfilling prophesy in March, 1622 when the Pohatan confederacy launched an uprising that targeted numerous English settlements. This spasm of violence took a fearful toll on the English colonists who suffered over 347 deaths, or roughly a third of the population.[271] The reprisals were calculating and equally brutal. The English in Virginia even convened a mock peace conference where they proceeded to poisoned over fifty of the attending Indians.[272] The news of the frightening events in Virginia was quickly disseminated to the Plymouth colony and to interested parties back in England by that summer. The immediate consequence was a redoubled incentive to remain prepared and vigilant. In the

---

[269] Richard Bagwell, *Ireland Under the Tudors: With a Succinct Account of the Earlier History*, vol. II (London: Longmans, Green, and Co, 1885), 161-166.

[270] Karen Ordahl Kupperman, "English Perceptions of Treachery, 1583-1640: The Case of the American 'Savages'," *The Historical Journal*, 20, no. 2 (June, 1977), 265.

[271] Frederick J. Fausz , "The First Act of Terrorism in English America" for History News Network, October, 2006. (accessed April 12, 2008); Kupperman, 269.

[272] Karr, 889.Fausz. There is some disagreement regarding the number killed by poisoning versus those slain by hand during the same conference.

long term, this native treachery increased the English wariness toward their Indian neighbors. Many of the English colonists in New England and the mother country accepted Captain John Smith's recommendations for dealing with the Indians. In short, he urged that the English in the New World should inspire fear and awe in the Indians as the most effective method for ensuring security.[273]

In 1636 when it appeared that the relative peace between the English and Indians might be fraying, the English decided that a strong military response was the most appropriate course of action to secure their position in the New England. The English were pragmatic and conservative in their assessment of their strategic position in New England. They feared that allowing the Oldham and Stone murders to go unpunished would encourage further similar behavior, or perhaps even inviting a wide scale uprising.[274] Conducting a retaliatory act against the Indians was consistent with native norms of conflict. The ferocity of the response however, was not. It was consistent with the norms of English practice against rebels, infidels, and criminals, or in other words- savages.

Once the expedition was underway, the English had committed themselves to war with the Indians. Lieutenant Lion Gardiner, a professional soldier, understood this even if John Endicott and his political masters in Boston did not. Gardiner possessed an understanding of the nature of war describing it beyond the terms of justice and punishment. Endicott's mission disturbed Gardiner since he feared that the action would incite rather than humble the Indians. He railed at the Bay Colony men, "…you come

---

[273] Cave, 14-15.
[274] Cave, 108-109.

hither to raise these wasps about my ears and then you will take wing and flee away..."[275]

The Indians responded as Gardiner had feared and this motivated the English to put an end to the rebelliousness of the Pequot. The English had attempted to deliver their demands to the Pequot. The Pequot had refused to comply. The English viewed this refusal by the Pequot as rebelliousness. As Karr explains, "In the eyes of the Puritan leaders, the Pequot, whatever their legal status, had become virtual subjects. And in dealing with lawless subjects, European military tradition was clear."[276] The conditions were set for the English to deliver a blow that would destroy the Pequot as a factor in the politics and settlement of Southern New England.

In their campaign against the Pequot the English set out to punish a people they viewed as insolent and dangerous; deserving destruction as Underhill justified, "…sometimes the Scripture declareth [sic] women and children must perish with their parents; sometime the case alters: but we will not dispute it now."[277] The military force sent against them fought with a certainty that their cause was just and that the Indians were irredeemable, rebels, and infidels. The English set out to subjugate their enemies, with a level of ferocity familiar to Europeans of the period. They overmatched the Indians in the tools of war. More importantly, they possessed the refined ruthlessness to use those tools against an entire people. In their response, the Indians met the English in their traditional ways, with their traditional weapons and found themselves overmatched. The proud Pequot were first defeated, then pursued, finally cornered and destroyed as an independent people.

---

[275] Lion Gardener, "*A History of the Pequot War 1660,*" (Cincinnati: J Harpel, 1860), 10-12.
[276] Karr, 908; Underhill, 13-14.
[277] Underhill, 36.

CHAPTER 6

CONCLUSION

The Puritan World-View As The Force Behind The War

Compromise and accommodation were never part of the English long-term agenda for the Pequot Indians of southern New England. The hard experiences of the Puritans in the crucible of European political and religious struggle shaped their sense of purpose and their responses to the world around them. The Puritan devotion to an interpretation of the Christian faith was the underpinning for all aspects of their civic culture and informed their decision-making. Their ideological perspective guided the actions of the English Puritans in dealing with the Pequot, and other tribes.

That Puritan ideological view was decidedly exclusive. Their vision for expansion assumed a conversion of neighboring tribes. Pequot resistance to the imposition of European ideals and norms set them in opposition to the English and on a path to conflict, a conflict the Pequot could not win. That short but bloody war eclipsed what compromise had come before and foreshadowed the pattern of Indian and European-American relations for next two hundred and fifty years.

The Puritan militias that fought against the Pequot represented only the first probing advances of a society with a potent military culture. English military leadership in the colonies was indoctrinated in a sophisticated and ruthless practice of organized violence.[278] They communicated this to the novice colonial volunteers with sufficient skill to make the militia a lethal opponent to the indigenous people.

However, it is important to note that English military superiority at the time of the Pequot War is not simply a matter of Europeans with firearms pitted against a technologically backward opponent. The brutal nature of the violence that erupted between the English and the Pequot highlights the profound differences between the military cultures of the two societies. The native people of New England operated within a self-moderating system of almost ritualistic limited violence.[279] The Europeans of the same period also operated in a highly ritualized military culture, however, the European military system was oriented toward large-scale combat often marked by mass violence and calculated atrocity. The technological advantages enjoyed by the Europeans in terms of protection, firearms, and steel weapons contributed to this military mismatch but should not stand alone as a reason for the annihilation of the Pequot.

The English who established colonies in Massachusetts Bay, Plymouth, and Connecticut were subject to an understanding of the world dominated by a 17th century Protestant conceit that allowed them to equate their mission in North America with the Biblical accounts of the Hebrew conquest of Canaan. This provided a pretext for a total war against an entire people. The Pequot, diminished by disease, divided by politics, and threatened by native neighbors and Europeans became surrogate Canaanites. They represented at once a spiritual and physical challenge for the Puritans to overcome.

---

[278] Geoffrey Parker. "Dynastic War", In *The Cambridge History of Warfare*, Geoffrey Parker, ed. (New York: Cambridge University Press, 2005), 148-150.
[279] Thomas Morton; Hirsch, 1190.

In this context, relatively minor events, like the murders of John Stone and John Oldham, became the tinder for a war of annihilation. What the practical demands of commerce had brought into proximity, the absolute requirements of religion brought into conflict. It was not simply the lure of more land, or the monopoly of markets, since those outcomes would transpire with conversion, absorption and subsequent "civilization".[280] It was the perceived resistance of the Pequot to the Puritan objectives of colonization and conversion that set the two peoples on a path of collision. The Puritan understanding of their mission, as described by their clergy and elected leaders did not allow for a middle ground of compromise.

The Pequot were offered terms, as far as the Puritans could move toward compromise with an uncivilized people and not violate their own obedience before their God.[281] If those terms, or conditions, were not acceptable then the Puritans considered themselves justified in taking the path of war. The Puritans then turned to the pages of the Old Testament just as much as they turned to the military writings of their contemporaries for guidance on how to deal with the new Canaanites.[282] Finally, they moved to subjugate their foes and remove them as an obstacle, and a threat to their settlement of the land opened to them, so they believed, by the providence of God.

---

[280] Author Lynn Ceci has asserted that the Massachusetts Bay Colony sought to dominate the wampum producing areas of southern New England and that this was a key motivation for the war. This idea is not well supported when considering the ideological underpinnings of Puritan actions; See also Alfred A. Cave, *The Pequot War*, (Amherst, MA: University of Massachusetts Press, 1996, 5.

[281] See Governor John Winthrop's "A Model of Christian Charity" sermon. John Winthrop, "A Model of Christian Charity", John Beardsley, ed. http://religiousfreedom.lib. virginia.edu/sacred /charity.html, (accessed February 14, 2008). He gives a warning that if the Puritans deal falsely, or fail to follow the path God has laid for them then they could rightly expect punishment as is often described in scripture, particularly the Old Testament examples. This is a frequent exhortation in Puritan writings from the period.

[282] Parker, 157. ; Tudor. 38.

By extinguishing the Pequot as a factor in southern New England, the English communicated their ruthlessness to the other tribes. It removed, for a short period, a feeling of vulnerability for the colonies.[283] The war also established a precedent for action against other tribes both in New England and beyond. The reality, evident in the aftermath, was that the native people had only two real options. They could assimilate and be absorbed by the English or they could resist. The path of resistance ultimately meant war with the English and if the fate of the Pequot demonstrated nothing else it demonstrated that the English would be predatory and ruthless in the execution of their policies and punishment of those who opposed them.

Indians who had joined with the English to defeat the Pequot discovered that their position was not improved in the long term. Leaders among the tribes, notably Uncas of the Mohegan tribe, supplicated themselves to the English in a vain hope that they might retain a measure of sovereignty. Each compromise or arrangement with the English colonists marked a diminution of their freedom. Their distrust of the English festered. The English suspicions soon returned to the forefront and they again confronted the specters of Indian savagery and ill intentions toward the Christian colonists.[284]

The treaty ending the war in 1638 communicated in concrete terms English sovereignty over Southern New England.[285] The English assumed greater liberties to arbitrate disputes, modify treaties, and enforce English laws.[286] The leadership in

---

[283] Kupperman, 270.
[284] Cave, 162-163.
[285] Cave, 162.
[286] Cave, 163. Courts and Commissions in the Massachusetts Bay Colony and in Connecticut dealt with local tribes as subjects not independent nations. These bodies issued demands for arrest, trial, and in some cases, execution of Indians "convicted" of legal violations. In the years following the Pequot War and

Massachusetts Bay continued to interpret their role in New England in terms largely consistent with the Winthrop's stated vision for their society.[287] English dominance over their promised land continued to expand.

The English Puritans were rational men striving to build a life along the frontiers of civilization. Their ideas about the reality they left behind in Europe and the reality they encountered in North America reflected the sum of their accepted knowledge. They armed themselves with ideas and arguments derived from centuries of European experience, just as much as they did with weapons and armor. Their self awareness did not encompass many of the views on religion, race, and economics that developed in the centuries following their settlement in North America.

Modern arguments of racism and economics attempt to diminish the dominance of religion as an ideology of the absolute. Biases and agendas can manipulate theological views that interpret individual acts as divinely inspired and directed with profound impacts. Therefore, consideration of religion should not be discounted as a secondary concern if the religion in question underpins social, political and economic thought. The role of religion within a culture is often that of an ideological force which frames understanding, and shapes responses. Furthermore, fervent religious belief as a political force is not alien to our Western tradition or American history. Bringing this factor into consideration aids in the understanding the context of complex and multilayered historical events. Additionally this understanding gives us a basis for honest self-examination and perhaps a less biased analysis of other cultures today.

---

leading up to the King Phillips War of 1676 the enforcement of an English legal code was the clearest sign of the erosion of Indian sovereignty.

[287] Wertenbaker, 97; Cave, 172.

BIBLIOGRAPHY

Apess, William. *On Our Own Ground, The Complete Writings of William Apess, a Pequot 1620-1647.* Edited by Barry O'Connell. Amherst: University of Massachusetts Press, 1992.

Axtell, James. *The Invasion Within, the Contest of Cultures in Colonial North America.* New York: Oxford University Press, 1985.

Abbot, Jacob. *Abbot's American Histories.* Vol. I, *Aboriginal America.* New York: Sheldon and Company, 1860.

Bagwell, Richard. *Ireland Under the Tudors: With a Succinct Account of the Earlier History.* Vol. II. London: Longmans, Green, and Co. 1885. http://books.google.com /books (accessed January 3, 2008).

Boorstin, Daniel J. *The Americans, The Colonial Experience.* New York: Random House, 1958.

Bradford, William. *Of Plymouth Plantation, 1620-1647.* Edited by Samuel Eliot Morison. New York: Alfred A. Knopf Inc., 1970.

──── *Governor William Bradford's Letter Book.* Bedford Massachusetts: Bedford Books, 2001.

Burton, William and Richard Lowenthal. "The First of the Mohegans." *American Ethnologist,* Vol. 1, no. 4 (November 1974): 589-599.

Bushnell, Amy T. *Journal of Interdisciplinary History,* Vol. 27, no. 4 (Spring 1997): 712-713.

Byington, Ezra Hoyt. *The Puritan in England and New England.* Cambridge: University Press, 1896.

Cave, Alfred A., *The Pequot War*, Amherst, MA: University of Massachusetts Press, 1996.

──── "Who Killed John Stone? A Note on the Origins of the Pequot War." *The William and Mary Quarterly*, 3rd Ser., Vol. 49, No. 3 (July 1992): 509-521.

www.jstor.org/ (accessed October 10, 2007).

Canny, Nicholas ."Spenser's Irish Crisis: Humanism and Experience in the 1590s." *Past and Present*, No. 120 (August 1988): 201-209.

Chet, Guy. *Conquering the American Wilderness-The Triumph of European Warfare in the Colonial Northeast.* Amherst, MA: University of Massachusetts Press, 2003.

Cotton, John. "Gods Promise to His Plantation (1630)." Edited by Reiner Smolinski. http://digitalcommons.unl.edu/etas/22/ (accessed January 11, 2008).

Cronon, William. *Changes in the Land: Indians, Colonists, and the Ecology of New England.* New York: Hill and Wang, 1983.

Diamond, Jared. *Guns, Germs, And Steel, The Fates of Human Societies.* New York: W.W. Norton and Company, 1999.

Dowd, Roger, *The Pequots in Southern New England: The Rise and Fall of an American Indian Nation.* Norman and London: University of Oklahoma Press, 1990. http://www.dowdgen.com/dowd/document/pequots.html [accessed 10 January, 2008].

Elson, William Henry, "Rhode Island and Providence Plantation*,"* in *The History of the United States of America,* **(**Macmillan Company, New York, 1904) transcribed by Kathy Leigh**,** http://www.usahistory.info/New-England/Rhode-Island.html (accessed November 10, 2007).

Gardener, Lion. *A History of the Pequot War 1660.* Cincinnati: J Harpel, 1860.

———— *Relation of the Pequot Warres.* Hartford: Hartford Press, 1901.

Gratus, Hugo. *On the Law of War and Peace,1625.* Translated by A. C. Campbell, London: 1814. http://www.constitution.org/gro/djbp.htm (accessed January 4, 2008).

Hauptman, Laurence M. and Wherry, James D. *The Pequots in Southern New England:The Rise and Fall of an American Indian Nation.* Norman and London: University of Oklahoma Press, 1990.

Hayden, Mary Teresa. *A Short History of the Irish People from the Earliest Times to 1920.* London: Longmans, Green and Co., 1922.

Hirsch, Adam J. 1988. "The Collision of Military Cultures in Seventeenth-Century New England." *The Journal of American History,* Vol. 74, no. 4 (March 1988): 1187-1212. www.jstor.org/ (accessed December 10, 2007).

James, Sydney V., ed. *The New England Puritans*. New York: Harper and Row Publishers, 1968.

Jenks, Tudor. *Captain Myles Standish.* New York: Century Company, 1905.

Jennings, Francis. "Virgin Land and Savage People." *American Quarterly*, Vol. 23, No. 4 (October 1971):519-541. www.jstor.org/ (accessed November 8, 2007).

Johnson, Edward. *Wonder-Working Providence of Sions Savior in New England*. Edited by J. Franklin Jameson. New York: Charles Schribner and Sons, 1910. http://books. google.com/books (accessed January 21, 2008).

Louis Jordan, "The Dutch in America: From Discovery to the First Settlement, 1609-1621," http://www.coins.nd.edu/ColCoin/ColCoinIntros/NNHistory.html (accessed November 10, 2007).

Karr, Ronald D. "Why Should You Be So Furious? The Violence of the Pequot War." *The Journal of American History,* Vol. 85, no. 3 (December1998): 876-909. www.jstor.org/ (accessed November 15, 2007).

Kupperman, Karen Ordahl. "English Perceptions of Treachery, 1583-1640: The Case of the American 'Savages'." *The Historical Journal*, Vol. 20, No. 2 (June 1977): 263-287. www.jstor.org/ (accessed November 10, 2007).

Lane, Ralph. "The Colony at Roanoke" 1586. http://www.nationalcenter.org/ColonyofRoanoke.html (accessed January 18, 2008).

Lepore, Jill. *The Name of War King Philip's War and the Origins of American Identity.* New York: Knopf, 1998.

Maxwell, Richard Howland. "Religious Controversies." Pilgrim Society Note, Series Two, (June 1996): http://www.pilgrimhall.org/PSNoteNewReligious Controversies.ht (accessed October 11 2007).

Miller, Perry. *The New England Mind, From Colony to Province.* Boston: Beacon Press, 1953.

———— "The Puritan Way of Life." In *Puritanism in Early America,* edited by George M. Waller. Boston: DC Heath and Company, 1950, 4-19.

Mason, John. " A Brief History of the Pequot War*:* Especially of the Memorable Taking of their Fort at Mistick in Connecticut in 1637". In *Major Problems in American Military History*. Edited by John W. Chambers II and G.Kurt Piehler. Boston and New York: Houghton Mifflin Company, 1999, 7-10.

————*A Brief History of the Pequot War***:** *Especially of the Memorable Taking of their Fort at Mistick in Connecticut in 1637.* Boston: Keeland and T. Green, 1736. http://books. google.com/books (accessed February 10, 2008).

Morton, Thomas. "Manners and Customs of the Indians (of New England) 163." In *The Library of Original Sources.* Vol. V, *9th to 16th Centuries.* Edited by Oliver J. Thatcher. Milwaukee: University Research Extension Co., 1907. http://www.fordham.edu/halsall/mod/1637morton.html (accessed August 28, 2007).

Newman, Albert Henry. *A Manual of Church History.* Vol II, *Modern Church History (1517-1903).* Philadelphia: American Baptist Publication Society, 1903. http://books. google.com/books. (accessed February 10, 2008).

Osgood, Herbert L. *The American Colonies in the 17th Century.* Vol III. New York: MacMillan Company, 1907. http://books.google.com/books (accessed December 12, 2008).

Parker, Geoffrey. "Dynastic War." In *The Cambridge History of Warfare*, edited by Geoffrey Parker, New York: Cambridge University Press, 2005.

Pearce, Roy Harvey. "The Ruines of Mankind: The Indian and the Puritan Mind." *Journal of the History of Ideas*, Vol. 13, No. 2 (April 1952): 200-217. www.jstor.org/ (accessed November 12, 2007).

Philbrick, Nathaniel. *Mayflower, A Story of Courage Community and War.* London: Viking Penguin Group, 2006.

Pratt, Phinius. "Account of the Wessagussett Plantation." Edited by Marcia Stewart. ushttp://www.winthropsociety.org/home.php (accessed January 4, 2008).

Radune, Richard. *Pequot Plantation-The Story of an Early Colonial Settlement.* (Branford, Connecticut: Research in Time Publications, 2005).

Schaff, Phillip. *History of the Christian Church.* Volume VIII, *Modern Christianity. The Swiss Reformation.1882.* Christian Classics Ethereal Library, 2002. http:// www. ccel. org/ccel/schaff/hcc8.html 9 (accessed February 8, 2008).

Seed, Patricia. "The Conquest of the Americas." In *The Cambridge History of Warfare*. Edited by Geoffrey Parker. New York: Cambridge University Press, 2005.

Smith, John, "A Description of New England (1616)"*,* Paul Royster, ed., An Online Electronic Text Edition, http://digitalcommons.unl.edu/etas/4/ (accessed November 8, 2007).

Simmons, William S. "Cultural Bias in the New England Puritans' Perception of Indians." *The William and Mary Quarterly,* 3rd Ser., Vol. 38, no. 1 (January 1981): 56-72. www.jstor.org/ (accessed January 18, 2007).

Spenser, Edmund. *A Veue of the present state of Irelande.* [1596], prepared from the text found in Grosart [1894] The University of Oregon, 1997 http://www.uoregon.edu/~rbear/veue1.html (accessed January 12, 2008).

Sylvester, Herbert Milton. *Indian Wars of New England.* Vol I. Boston: The Everett Press, 1910.

Vaughan, Alden T. "Pequots and Puritans: The Causes of the War of 1637." *The William and Mary Quarterly,* Vol.21, no. 2 (April 1964): 256-269. www.jstor.org/ (accessed November 18 2007).

Vaughan, Alden T. "Expulsion of the Salvages: English Policy and the Virginia Massacre of 1622." *The William and Mary Quarterly*, 3rd Ser., Vol. 35, No. 1 (January 1978): 57-84. www.jstor.org/ (accessed December 5, 2007).

Underhill, John. "*Newes from America; Or, A New and Experimentall Discoverie of New England; Containing, A Trve Relation of Their War-like Proceedings These Two Yeares Last Past, with a Figure of the Indian Fort, or Palizado.*" Edited by Paul Royster. www.digitalcommons.unl.edu/etas/37/ (accessed October 24, 2007).

——— "Captain John Underhill Justifies the Attack on Mystic Village in the Pequot War (1637) ." In *Major Problems in American Military History.* Edited by John W Chambers II and G.Kurt Piehler. Boston and New York: Houghton Mifflin Company, 1999:41.

Verrazano, Giovanni. "Written Record of the Voyage of 1524 of Giovanni da Verrazano as recorded in a letter to Francis I, King of France, July 8th*,* 1524.**"** Edited by Lawrence C. Wroth. *The Voyages of Giovanni da Verrazzano, 1524-1528.* (Yale, 1970): 133-143. http://bc.barnard.columbia.edu/~ lgordis/earlyAC/documents/verrazan.htm (accessed 8 November 2007).

Vincent, Phillip. "A True Relation of the Late Battell fought in New England, between the English and the Salvages: With the present state of things there (1637)." Edited by Paul Royster. www.digitalcommons.unl.edu/etas/35/ (accessed September 15, 2007).

Weir, David A. "The Rhetoric and Ethnography of Prejudice." *American Quarterly,* Vol. 39, no. 3 (autumn 1987): 461-466.

Wertenbaker, Thomas J. *The First Americans 1607-1690.* Chicago: Quadrangle Books, 1955.

Whisker, James B., *Arms Makers of Colonial America.* London and Toronto: Associated University Press, 1992. http://books.google.com/books (accessed April 11, 2008).

Williams, Roger. "A Key into the Language of America." In *Major Problems in American Military History.* Edited by John W. Chambers II and Kurt G. Piehler. Boston and New York: Houghton Mifflin Company, 1999, 45-46.

―――― "A Key into the Language of America: Or an Help to the Language of the Natives, in that part of America, called New England. Together with brief Observations of the Customs, Manners, and Worships, &c. of the aforesaid Natives, in Peace and War, in Life and Death." Collections of the Massachusetts Historical Society, Vol.III, Boston : Apollo Press, http://capecodhistory.us/19th/MHS1794.htm#2039 [accessed January 4, 2008].

Winthrop, John. *The History of New England From 1630 to 1649.* Vol. 1. Edited by James Kendal Hosmer. New York: Scribner and Sons, 1908.

―――― "A Model of Christian Charity." Edited by John Beardsley. http://religiousfreedom.lib. virginia.edu/sacred /charity.html (accessed February 14, 2008).

――――-"Reasons for the Plantation in New England ca.1628."Edited by Marcia Elaine Stewart. http://www.winthropsociety.org/doc_reasons.php (accessed February 14, 2008).

Young, Alexander. *Chronicles of the Pilgrim Fathers of the Colony of Plymouth from 1602 to 1625.* Boston: Charles C. Little and James Brown, 1841. http://books.google.com/books (accessed December 12, 2007).

Made in the USA
Middletown, DE
10 July 2017